Cambridge Elements

Elements in Politics and Society in East Asia
edited by
Erin Aeran Chung
Johns Hopkins University
Mary Alice Haddad
Wesleyan University
Benjamin L. Read
University of California, Santa Cruz

JAPAN AS A GLOBAL MILITARY POWER

New Capabilities, Alliance Integration, Bilateralism-Plus

Christopher W. Hughes
University of Warwick

Shaftesbury Road, Cambridge CB2 8EA, United Kingdom

One Liberty Plaza, 20th Floor, New York, NY 10006, USA

477 Williamstown Road, Port Melbourne, VIC 3207, Australia

314–321, 3rd Floor, Plot 3, Splendor Forum, Jasola District Centre, New Delhi – 110025, India

103 Penang Road, #05–06/07, Visioncrest Commercial, Singapore 238467

Cambridge University Press is part of Cambridge University Press & Assessment, a department of the University of Cambridge.

We share the University's mission to contribute to society through the pursuit of education, learning and research at the highest international levels of excellence.

www.cambridge.org
Information on this title: www.cambridge.org/9781108971478

DOI: 10.1017/9781108975025

When citing this work, please include a reference to the DOI 10.1017/9781108975025

First published 2022

A catalogue record for this publication is available from the British Library.

ISBN 978-1-108-97147-8 Paperback
ISSN 2632-7368 (online)
ISSN 2632-735X (print)

Japan as a Global Military Power

New Capabilities, Alliance Integration, Bilateralism-Plus

Elements in Politics and Society in East Asia

DOI: 10.1017/9781108975025
First published online: August 2022

Christopher W. Hughes
University of Warwick

Author for correspondence: Christopher W. Hughes, c.w.hughes@warwick.ac.uk.

Abstract: Japan is emerging as a more prominent global and regional military power, defying traditional categorisations of a minimalist contribution to the US-Japan alliance, maintaining anti-militarism, seeking an internationalist role, or carving out more strategic autonomy. Instead, this Element argues that Japan has fundamentally shifted its military posture over the last three decades and traversed into a new categorisation of a more capable military power and integrated US ally. This results from Japan's recognition of its fundamentally changing strategic environment that requires a new grand strategy and military doctrines. The shift is traced across the national security strategy components of Japan Self-Defence Forces' capabilities, US-Japan alliance integration, and international security cooperation. The Element argues that all these components are subordinated inevitably to the objectives of homeland security and re-strengthening the US-Japan alliance, and thus Japan's development as international security partner outside the ambit of the bilateral alliance remains stunted. This title is also available as Open Access on Cambridge Core.

Keywords: Japan, military, Japan Self-Defence Forces, US-Japan alliance, international cooperation

ISBNs: 9781108971478 (PB), 9781108975025 (OC)
ISSNs: 2632-7368 (online), 2632-735X (print)

Contents

1 Introduction: Japan's New Military Profile

The Japan Self-Defence Forces (JSDF), just over thirty years ago in 1991, undertook its first tentative overseas despatch in the post-war period, taking the form of a small Maritime Self-Defence Force (MSDF) non-combat mine-sweeping mission to the Persian Gulf in the wake of the 1990–1 Gulf War. In the intervening three decades, Japan's global military engagement has extended ever further outwards geographically from the Asia-Pacific and Indo-Pacific to the Middle East, Africa, and Europe. The JSDF's scope of operations as made clear in the revised 2018 National Defence Programme Guidelines (NDPG) – the document that lays out Japan's military doctrine alongside the necessary force structure – has also expanded beyond the traditional land, sea, and air domains and into the outer space, cyber, and electromagnetic domains (JMOD 2018). The JSDF has further expanded its range of operations functionally to involve United Nations peacekeeping operations (UNPKO), counter-piracy missions, maritime security, logistical support, and potentially since 2015, following the passage of a raft of new 'peace and security legislation', collective self-defence combat missions.

Japan's range of partners and frameworks for military cooperation has also grown to now encompass not just the United States as its bilateral security treaty and alliance partner, but new partners in multinational coalitions, multilateral institutions, and new 'quasi-allies' such as Australia. Japan has manoeuvred itself, for instance, to be at the core of the Quadrilateral Security Dialogue (Japan hosting its summit in May 2022), or so-called Quad, involving itself, the United States, India, and Australia, and the concept of the Free and Open Indo-Pacific (FOIP), that contain a focus on maritime military cooperation.

Moreover, Japan's rise and credibility as a global military power has been supported by the incremental but nevertheless relentless build-up of the JSDF's capabilities. The MSDF, Air Self-Defence Force (ASDF), and Ground Self-Defence Force (GSDF) have long possessed considerable capabilities for Japan's own immediate territorial defence and to provide a defensive complement to the United States's offensive power capabilities stationed in and around Japan in a classic 'shield' and 'spear' division of labour. In more recent years, though, the JSDF has sought to augment its capabilities by investing in advanced military technologies and hardware, to move towards more jointness of inter-service operations with the United States, and to acquire its own mobile and flexible forces able to project power. The JSDF inventory now includes an Amphibious Rapid Deployment Brigade (ARDB), amphibious ships, a force of eight ballistic missile defence (BMD)-capable *Aegis* destroyers with further maritime BMD assets slated, helicopter carriers, destroyers converted to 'defensive' fixed-wing aircraft carriers, the largest force of F-35 fighter aircraft outside the US Air Force (USAF), in-flight refuelling, unmanned aerial and underwater vehicles, joint direct-attack munitions, air-launched stand-off missiles, intelligence satellites, and the probable procurement of cruise missiles and hyper-velocity gliding projectiles (HVGP). All these developments would suggest that Japan can become a more reliable alliance partner, work more effectively with new partners, and deploy force outside its own territory and possibly outside the traditional defensive 'shield' role to apply its own element of counter-strike power.

Furthermore, Japan's enhanced military presence has been reinforced by a seemingly new strategic and political intent to mobilise and utilise its military capabilities for international security ends. Prime Minister Abe Shinzō's administration, from 2012 to 2020, in creating Japan's first ever National Security Strategy (NSS) and National Security Council (NSC) famously propounded the concept of a 'proactive contribution to peace'. According to the NSS, Japan would:

> As a major player in the world politics and the economy, contribute even more proactively in securing peace, stability, and prosperity of the international community, while achieving its own security as well as peace and stability in the Asia-Pacific region, as a "Proactive Contributor to Peace" based on the principle of international cooperation (Cabinet Secretariat 2013).

The administration of Prime Minister Suga Yoshihide, from 2020 to 2021, maintained the policy of a proactive contribution to peace, repeating its centrality in international fora such as the UN General Assembly and in domestic settings to reassure the public over Japan's security direction (Suga 2020). Kishida Fumio, the new prime minister from the end of 2021, was a major advocate of the policy during his previous service as Japan's longest-serving foreign minister in the post-war era from 2012 to 2017 (MOFA 2016a). Kishida's own concepts, articulated in 2022, of a 'Vision for Peace' and 'realism diplomacy for a new era' essentially continue the policy trajectory of Abe in security and defence (Kishida 2022).

This declared intent on Japan's part has been backed up by the steady removal or de facto hollowing out of many of the constitutional constraints and anti-militaristic principles that in the past were assessed as both symbolic and substantive limits on its military ambitions and external commitments. Japan's procurement of long-range missiles, in-flight refuelling, and aircraft carriers has challenged its public pledge throughout the post-war period 'not to become a great military power' (*gunji taikoku to naranai*). The Japanese government in recent years has effectively overturned bans in 2008 on the peaceful use of space for military purposes, in 2014 on the export of arms and military technology and the institution instead of the Three Principles on the Transfer of Defence Equipment and Technology, and in 2017 the 1 per cent of GDP limit on defence expenditure (Hughes 2022; Hornung 2020a: 8–9). Most significantly, in 2014 Japan lifted its ban, in place since the early 1950s, on the exercise of collective self-defence (Hughes 2017).

In turn, Japan's new capabilities and statements of intent have raised enhanced expectations from its partners that it can play a pivotal and ever more forthcoming role in cooperating to consolidate the existing regional and global security orders. Washington DC policymakers have long regarded Japan's alignment with US military strategy as the 'cornerstone' for the maintenance of the entire regional security architecture, and constantly sought a more proactive Japanese military contribution to the alliance, and for Japan to support other US alliance partners in the region. Japan's perceived increasing activism is thus welcomed by the United States, and the new Joseph R. Biden administration has moved to further strengthen US-Japan alliance ties. The March 2021 Security Consultative Committee (SCC) statement, April 2021 Joint Leaders' Statement, January 2022 SCC statement, and May 2022 US-Japan Summit (MOFA 2022b) recommitted Japan and the United States to the FOIP, Quad, and 'rules-based international order', to deepen defence cooperation across all domains, further cooperation with US allies and partners, and to prevent China from challenging the status quo in the region (MOFA 2021a, 2021b, MOFA 2022a).

At the same time, other regional and global partners – through fora such as the Quad, FOIP, ASEAN, and recently signed bilateral strategic partnerships and dialogues with states as far afield as the United Kingdom, France, European Union (EU), and North Atlantic Treaty Organisation (NATO) – have similarly built expectations that Japan can become a more active and reciprocal military partner. A truly more proactive Japan, with its highly professional JSDF and full array of technologically advanced military capabilities placed at the disposal of existing and new allies, partners, and frameworks, would provide for a formidable strengthening of the international security order, particularly at a time when it is under strain following Russia's invasion of Ukraine in early 2022. Conversely, Japan's moves to strengthen its military activity outside its traditional confines are clearly of major interest not only to potential partners but also to potential adversaries such as China and North Korea.

1.1 Making Sense of Japan's Security Trajectory

As Japan continues to change shape and to stretch its presence in terms of geographical reach, traditional and non-traditional domains, functions, partners and frameworks, capabilities, and declared intent, the question is raised, therefore, of how to interpret the trajectory and significance of these new global military ambitions. Not unsurprisingly, given the inherently controversial nature of Japan's military role in the post-war period, there is no consensus in international and domestic policymaking and academic circles.

Many prevalent strains of analysis of Japan's expansion and diversification of military commitments have tended to frame developments as a continuation of, and gradual adjustment within, the still dominant post-war patterns of security policy, often seen as essentially a four-fold categorisation derived from the interplay of the degrees to which Japan is willing to utilise force for security and to align itself with the United States (Samuels 2006: 116–17). Japan, for the first and still majority strain of analysis, is viewed as essentially adhering or defaulting, with some modifications, to the post-war grand strategy designed by Prime Minister Yoshida Shigeru (1946–7, 1948–54) and his successors, or the so-called 'Yoshida Doctrine'. This line is characterised by a minimalist defence posture, dependence on the United States for security, and prioritisation of economic interests (Samuels 2003, 2007; Pyle 2007). If Japan is expanding its military presence, then it is still within the confines of this strategic paradigm (Green 2001; Oros 2008, 2017; Liff 2015; Smith 2019; Hagström and Williamson 2009), remains highly cautious in approach, and is a presence and role largely designed to be creating new partners and frameworks to continue its traditional hedging tactics of obviating alliance dilemmas of entrapment and abandonment vis-à-vis its US ally (Heginbotham and Samuels 2002).

This view of Japan as continuing to hew to the Yoshida line has some overlap with a second still influential strain of analyses that tend also towards arguing for essential continuity in security policy and are derived from an emphasis on the apparent ongoing influence of domestic anti-militaristic sentiment. Japan is regarded as still being heavily constrained in its military activities by attachment to a range of 'pacifist' or 'anti-militaristic' norms and identities derived from Article 9, or the so-called 'peace clause', of the 1946 promulgated constitution. Some analyses have tended to regard these norms as seemingly immutable (Berger 1993; Katzenstein and Okawara 1993; Le 2021) and strongly constraining Japan; others have seen norms and identities as more pliable and capable of shifting shape over time (Takao 2008; Hagström and Hanssen 2015; Hatakeyama 2021) to enable some tolerance of military power for national security ends if cast in the name of a contribution to international peace.

A third strain of analyses, again with some overlap with this view of 'pacifist' traditions, and to an extent buying into Japanese leaders' professed desire to contribute to international security, suggest that Japan has a relatively strong streak of internationalism and multilateralism in its strategic thinking (Singh 2008; Midford 2020). Hence, Japan, in reflecting its declared credentials as a liberal and democratic power, or 'middle power' (Soeya 2005), is now seeking to enhance its role in international security and work with multiple partners and institutions such as the United Nations (UN) (Dobson 2003) and beyond the bilateralism of the US-Japan alliance, either to complement ties with the United States and moderate its behaviour (Cha 2003), or to forge alternatives to the bilateral alliance to cope with dilemmas of entrapment and abandonment (Midford 2018), and even to lay the ground for new frameworks for regional and global security.

Finally, a fourth and periodically recurrent, but less prevalent, strain of analysis sees Japan's expansion of its global military profile as presaging enhanced strategic and diplomatic autonomy (*jishu gaikō*) or even full strategic independence. Japan is viewed as looping back to traditions of earlier strategic thought that argue for retaking its place as a great power as in the pre-war period. In line with this approach, Japan is seen as reaching out regionally and globally to initiate the types of free-flowing partnerships and alliances that might enable it to gradually detach itself from the United States, again, either as insurance against over-dependence on the United States (George Mulgan 2008), or to forge a strategic line that diverges from that of the United States (Fatton 2019).

All these interpretations offer some traction on thinking through Japan's growing global military presence. But none are sufficient individually, or even if taken in combination, to provide an accurate analysis. The contention that Japan is holding steady within the Yoshida Doctrine, adopting a minimalist military line, and still hedging as hard as in the past and especially against entrapment, appears at odds with the reality of its expanding military prowess and alliance commitments. The argument that Japan continues to be fundamentally constrained by domestic anti-militaristic sentiment struggles to convince in the face of the systematic dismantlement of nearly every post-war constitutional barrier and prohibition on the use of military power. Japan might be engaging with more partners than before and more multilateral frameworks, but the idea that this is designed as an 'internationalist' or principal thrust to its security policy, or an alternative to the US-Japan alliance, appears highly questionable. For it needs to be noted that Japan is devoting relatively limited military resources to many of these multilateral activities and is at pains to make sure that those multilateral efforts it does devote resources to usually include the

United States, support US strategy, do not in any way detract from the bilateral relationship, and are focussed on allies and partners of the United States. Finally, although Japan's desire for greater military autonomy is arguably part of the rhetoric and agenda of many of its leading policymakers, that this spells necessarily a desire for absolute strategic independence, and can be translated into a feasible option of moving away from the US-Japan alliance appears an unpersuasive position given the ever-deepening, and arguably inextricable, integration of bilateral military cooperation.

This Element, therefore, takes a different tack from many of these existing interpretations of Japan's emergent global military role. The argument is not to deny that these interpretations have utility but instead that it is necessary to progress beyond them to a more critical and effective synthesis, and to offer some sharply revised interpretations, and thus overall different conclusions on Japanese military trajectory. It takes sides with and goes somewhat beyond other literature that has been prepared for some time to argue against the received wisdom and point to new and more radical trajectories in Japan's military stance (Hughes 2004, 2009, 2015, 2016, 2017; Grönning 2014; Hornung 2014; Maslow 2015; Pyle 2018; Wilkins 2018a; Gustafsson, Hagström, and Hanssen 2018; Hughes, Patalano, and Ward 2021). Hence, this Element's take on Japan's military role is that there is far more change than continuity; that there is still some residual minimalism and hedging in approaching security policy and ties with the United States, but this is greatly outweighed by changing and ever deepening US-centred military cooperation; and anti-militarism still to a degree influences Japan's security debate but has been eroded to the point that it is no longer a fundamental determinant or roadblock for military policy. Similarly, Japan's internationalism and multilateralism have grown in quantity in certain instances but remain more nominal in quality and relatively limited in scope and substance, and very much subordinate and geared to support the objectives of the US-Japan alliance relationship at the core of Japan's security (Kawaski 2007: 78–9). In turn, the strength of this bilateralism means the impulse for a more autonomous Japanese security policy remains largely suppressed and is not yet a serious strategic objective.

In contrast to many of the dominant analyses to date, this Element argues that Japan's overriding motivation for seeking to change and engage in expanded security activities – whether geographical or functional in scope, or with new bilateral partners or multilateral frameworks – has always been and continues to be to find ways to conform with and ultimately reinforce the US-Japan alliance and US regional security presence for the defence of the Japanese homeland. Japan no longer easily fits the confines of the traditional post-war security categorisations: it is not significantly hedging, is increasingly less averse to considering the utility of military power in the toolbox of statecraft, is not seeking major multilateral alternatives to the bilateral alliance, and not focussing on attaining strategic autonomy. Instead, Japan is seeking more straightforwardly, and as should be readily apparent from empirical observation of trends in its military posture and its challenging security environment, to become an increasingly capable and reliable US ally. Japan's interest in the broader security of international society remains of relatively minor importance or even of insignificance at times. Japan's 'going global' in military affairs is thus a means not to 'de-centre' but to 're-centre' ultimately towards and reinforce the US security relationship and is dependent upon, constrained, and governed in its overall parameters by traditional bilateral alliance impulses. Japan as a global military power means in effect nothing other than becoming a more integrated US ally and working with other partners in and outside the Asia-Pacific or Indo-Pacific regions in a 'bilateralism-plus' mode, even if expanded in scope, that still takes its cue from US-Japan alliance priorities. The expectations of many other states for Japan to become a fully-fledged and reciprocal military partner outside this US-centred framework to assist with their own or wider global security concerns may thus prove limited or illusory.

This Element further explains not only the trajectory, qualities, and limitations but also the principal drivers behind Japan's emergence and direction as a global military power. Japan's evolving military stance is part of a broader shift in national grand strategy generated by changing international and domestic drivers, encapsulated by the 'Abe Doctrine' as elaborated by recently deceased Prime Minister Abe, and continuing to influence his successors, even if not explicitly using that terminology. The Abe Doctrine posits a more proactive security and military role for Japan but ultimately one that centres on a strengthened US-Japan alliance, with other forms of international military cooperation subordinated to bilateral alliance requirements.

The arguments of this Element are developed across four main sections. Section 2 traces Japan's changing strategic and military outlook across the post-war era and the ways in which post–Cold War new external threat perceptions and deep concern over the US's declining hegemonic military power, coupled with domestic political changes, have engineered a decisive shift in grand strategy – culminating in the Abe Doctrine – and over time fundamental changes in military posture. The outcome has been for Japan to talk of a new three-layered security strategy in the form of augmenting its own military capabilities, reinvesting in the US-Japan alliance, and newly exploring supplementary frameworks for international and multilateral cooperation.

Section 3 explores the transformation of defence doctrines and capabilities by the JSDF, making for a more muscular military stance. Japan's greatly enhanced capabilities in terms of the procurement of qualitatively advanced weapons systems, mobility, and joint operations are examined across the GSDF, ASDF, and MSDF, and in the domains of space, cyberspace, and electromagnetic warfare. The section explores trends in Japan's resourcing of its build-up of military systems, and the consideration of a strike option against overseas targets to now move potentially beyond defensive shield functions and acquire its own spear alongside the offensive power of the United States. The key argument is that Japan, in developing these formidable capabilities, is understandably gearing these ever more to the defence of the homeland against China and North Korea and for enhanced compatibility with the US military rather than for any broader international security role or attempt to establish autonomy from the bilateral alliance.

Section 4 analyses the US-Japan alliance and Japan's radically changing function and terms of engagement within it. The argument is made that Japan is seeking to 'double down' on support for the US-Japan alliance and has accepted that it must play a more active role to support its ally, now involving possibly fighting alongside the United States through collective self-defence, and that this involves a strengthened shield role but even, if necessary, a spear role, and the deeper and near inextricable integration of JSDF doctrines and capabilities with those of the United States. Japan is showing reduced inclination to hedge its alliance commitments and is inured to the fact that it now stands on the frontline of US military strategy in the region and might be obligated in attempts to defend the 'first island chain' in East Asia and encompassing Taiwan.

Section 5 investigates Japan's expanding military cooperation in international and multilateral frameworks and the degree of significance of these in its overall military posture. It argues that while Japan has upped the quantity of international cooperation in terms of geography, functions, and partners, much of the quality of cooperation is still limited in the relative degree of policy energy and resources devoted to it, is often legitimised, designed, and undertaken primarily to reinforce US-Japan alliance cooperation, and does not offer and is not seeking to lessen dependence on the United States. Japan thus continues its practice of essentially 'bilateralism-plus' in international security cooperation, as even with more 'plus' partnerships these still only serve as additions to reinforce the US-Japan alliance at the core rather than offer any deviation from its objectives.

2 Japan's Shifting Strategic and Military Outlook

Japan's formulation of its grand strategy for security and defence has undergone a radical shift in the post–Cold War period, often proceeding in incremental, even imperceptible, yet cumulatively significant steps, and at other times in rapid and major jolts forward. The drivers for this change in strategic trajectory have encompassed a range of external security challenges globally and regionally, and, correspondingly, evolving domestic frameworks for security policymaking and fundamental debates over Japan's international military commitments.

2.1 The Yoshida Doctrine as Grand Strategy

Japan's default grand strategy for much of the post-war era has been characterised by the Yoshida Doctrine. This grand strategy sought Japan's adaptation to the immediate and intense set of post-war challenges comprising absolute defeat in the Pacific War, occupation by US-led allied forces, promulgation in 1946 of the constitution and Article 9 'peace clause', general economic devastation, deep domestic fissures between the left and right politically over defence policy, and a hostile East Asia region due to the legacy of Japanese colonialism and rising Cold War tensions. Japan's resultant choice under Yoshida was alignment with the United States through the signing of the 1951 US-Japan security treaty, limited rearmament leading to the eventual establishment of the JSDF in 1954, and a focus on economic reconstruction. The 'pragmatist' successors of Yoshida in the mainstream of the Liberal Democratic Party (LDP) in power from 1955 onwards were then to evolve these choices into an effective, durable, and flexible strategic pathway (Dower 1988: 371–7; Samuels 2003: 203–11).

Japan in effect forged a grand strategic bargain with the United States under the security treaty, accepting the presence on its territory of US bases and forces to project power into the East Asia region in return for de facto – and then later under the revised 1960 security treaty, de jure – security guarantees. In turn, the Japanese pragmatists' choice of alignment with the United States helped to contain domestic political divides over security policy. The political left and 'pacifists', as the then second main competing strain of strategic thought, found mainly in the guise of the Japan Socialist Party (JSP) (later reforming as the Social Democratic Party of Japan (SDPJ) in 1996) and standing on an interpretation of Article 9 as prohibiting the maintenance of any military forces, opposed the US-Japan security treaty and advocated a policy of unarmed neutrality. But the fact that alignment with the United States and dependence on the superpower's security guarantees required only limited rearmament on the part of Japan deprived the left of many arguments about the risks of remilitarisation and antagonising East Asian states.

At the opposite political pole, the 'revisionist' or 'neo-autonomist' conservatives as the third strain of strategic thinking, and largely vested in the right of the

LDP, preferred a more independent security policy, free of foreign forces on Japanese territory, facilitating the formation of shifting alliances to respond to the changing balance of power, and significant national rearmament. Again, though, the decision to align with the United States proved tolerable for the revisionists as it indicated a willingness to respond to security challenges rather than retreat to pacifism and the prospect of Japan rebuilding its military power over the longer term.

Japan's chosen strategic pathway also offered possibilities for the fourth strain of strategic thinking that proposed a more East Asian region-centred, multilateral, and internationalist approach to security policy. Although alignment with the United States meant Japan's effective isolation from many East Asian states in the communist camp during the Cold War – Japan was unable to normalise ties with China and then sign a peace treaty until 1972 and 1978, and no peace treaty was signed with the USSR and still none with Russia to the present day – integration into the US-led international order provided a framework for Japan to rebuild ties with many newly independent states in the East Asia region and to sponsor entry into global institutions such as the UN.

The ability of the Yoshida Doctrine to respond to Japan's immediate external challenges and to contain and bridge many domestic strategic debates thus set it on the trajectory to dominate as grand strategy for much of the post-war era. This pathway was further consolidated and given longevity by its capability to flex continually in the face of new security demands.

Japan's security situation became more complex as the Cold War developed, with the steady rise of the Soviet threat in Northeast Asia and concomitantly US pressure for Japan to expand its security role in response. The Yoshida Doctrine underwent consequent adjustments. The revised 'mutual' 1960 security treaty not only made more explicit US obligations to defend Japan under Article 5, but also crucially in Article 6 pointed to the importance of the treaty to function for the wider peace and security of East Asia. Japan, in formulating the 1978 Guidelines for US-Japan Defense Cooperation, explored for the first time direct bilateral military cooperation with the United States under Article 6 of the security treaty to contribute to its own and wider regional security. Moreover, throughout the 1980s, the JSDF undertook a major quantitative and qualitative expansion of capabilities in response to the Soviet build-up, including an emphasis on GSDF main battle tanks (MBT) and artillery to counter any invasion in the northern island of Hokkaidō, the strengthening of the MSDF's destroyer fleet and anti-submarine warfare (ASW) capabilities, and the ASDF's upgrading of fighter interceptor capabilities. Through augmenting JSDF capabilities, Japan was providing for its own defence and starting also to create a complementary military division of labour with the United States, acting as the 'shield' to defend US forces in and around Japan and freeing up the United States to focus on the 'spear' of offensive power. The US-Japan security relationship developed to the point that in 1981, for the first time in the thirty years since the treaty's signing, Japan's leaders ventured to refer to it as an 'alliance' (*Nichibei dōmei*) (Tanaka 1997: 265–304).

Although the Yoshida Doctrine dominated post-war grand strategy and flexed to accommodate alliance demands, Japan's policymakers were conscious that attachment to it was not without risks and should not be unconditional. Japan's choice of alignment and then shift to alliance with the United States presented inherent dilemmas of entrapment and abandonment requiring constant calibration and management. The JSDF, as a case in point, whilst building up its capabilities, concentrated on systems that were designed solely for the defence of national land and sea space. Although these capabilities could act as a defensive shield for US forces in Japan, they were not integrated tactically or in command-and-control with the US military and were highly limited in their own power projection to avoid risks of involvement in US expeditionary warfare.

Japan's hedging through complementary but essentially separate forces from those of the United States was reinforced by the range of constitutional prohibitions and anti-militaristic principles derived from Article 9 of the constitution that minimised international and alliance security obligations and reassured regional neighbours, domestic political opposition, and the public over Japanese military intentions. Japan promoted an 'exclusively defence-oriented policy' (*senshu bōei*). Most crucially, since 1954, Japan held to the interpretation that whilst as a sovereign nation under the UN Charter it possesses the right to collective self-defence (*shūdan-teki jieiken*), the exercise of this right is prohibited by Article 9 of the Japanese constitution as exceeding the necessary use of force for individual self-defence (*kobetsu-teki jieiken*). Japan was barred from using armed force to assist its US ally or other states outside its own territory. Similarly, Japan expounded from 1967 the 'three non-nuclear principles' (not to produce, possess, or introduce nuclear weapons); a complete ban from 1976 onwards on the export of military technology (excepting a limited number of technological projects with the US); the 'peaceful' use of outer space from 1969; and from 1976 a 1 per cent GDP limit on defence expenditure. Individually and in combination, these principles made for a highly restrained military stance during the Cold War period, although none of them, despite originating from the spirit of the Japanese constitution, were legally binding, so allowing policymakers to maximise future strategic freedom (Hughes 2004).

2.2 Global and Regional Challenges to Japanese Strategy

If the Yoshida Doctrine proved dominant, durable, and flexible for much of the post-war era and Cold War period, then it has come under significant stress in the post–Cold War period to the point it can no longer be stretched effectively to meet extant international security challenges, or be squared with domestic political opinion, and has obliged policymakers to revisit fundamental assumptions over grand strategy. The first set of international challenges came on the global level in the wake of the Gulf War of 1990–1 as Japan was confronted by security issues that it had largely been insulated from by US military hegemony during the Cold War. Japan now faced expectations from its US ally and the international community to provide a 'human' contribution to the multinational war effort in the form of the overseas despatch of the JSDF. The Japanese government did attempt to despatch the JSDF to the Gulf region on non-combat logistical support missions, but these LDP efforts were blocked by the JSP and opposition parties, and even by the hesitancy of elements of the LDP itself. In the final event, Japan proved able only to provide a very significant financial contribution of US$13 billion to support the coalition forces. After the cessation of hostilities, Japan managed to despatch MSDF minesweepers to the Gulf in 1991, as noted at the start of this Element. Japanese moves overall were nevertheless still derided by many as 'chequebook diplomacy', and the perceived international critique of Japan's minimalist and low-risk response to this crisis reopened many of the domestic fissures around security policymaking. Japan eventually passed a new International Peace Cooperation Law (IPCL) in June 1992 to allow the despatch of the JSDF on non-combat UNPKO for the first time, and opening the way to further question post-war constraints on Japan's deployment of military power for national security ends.

Japan's grand strategy was further shaken on the global level by the events of 9/11 and the ensuing 'war on terror'. Japanese policymakers perceived the need to demonstrate solidarity with the United States and international community to expunge the threats of terrorism and weapons of mass destruction (WMD), and to do so through the despatch of the JSDF. Moreover, despite risks of entrapment in US-led expeditionary coalitions in the Indian Ocean and Gulf regions, policymakers calculated that Japan should demonstrate further proactivity and support to obviate the even greater risks of abandonment by the United States as an unreliable ally (Pyle 2018: 356–60).

The second set of international challenges to Japan's strategic outlook has been manifest increasingly on the regional level (Singh 2020: 66–100). Japanese regional concerns were focussed in the initial post–Cold War period on North Korea's nuclear and ballistic missile programmes, but have been rivalled and then superseded by China's rise and military modernisation. The North Korean nuclear crisis of 1993–4 provided a reality check for Japanese policymakers in exposing the US-Japan alliance's limitations for responding to regional contingencies. Japan's preference to concentrate under the 1978 Guidelines for US-Japan Defense Cooperation on Japan-focussed Article 5-type contingencies rather than bilateral cooperation for regional-focussed Article 6-type contingencies meant that it was unprepared to respond to US requests for military logistical support in the event of a conflict on the Korean Peninsula. The spectre was again raised of Japan's abandonment as an unreliable ally. Recurrent fears of abandonment have compounded Japan's growing concerns over North Korea since the mid-1990s. The principal anxiety is that the United States might not fulfil its security guarantees to Japan if North Korea acquires a nuclear strike and blackmail capability against US forces in the Asia-Pacific or the US homeland, a scenario of whether the United States would sacrifice Los Angeles for Tokyo.

Meanwhile, China's rising power has most significantly exacerbated Japan's strategic concerns. Japanese policymakers comprehend the inevitability of China's political and economic rise; the importance of Sino-Japanese economic interdependence for Japan's own prosperity; and the need to influence China's interaction with the international system (Mochizuki 2007). At the same time, Japan's policy elites have expressed anxieties over China's growing willingness to project military force in pursuit of its national interests and beyond its immediate territory. Japanese policymakers were first alerted to this challenge by the Taiwan Strait crisis of 1995–6, with the People's Liberation Army (PLA) conducting ballistic missile tests to intimidate Taiwan and close to Japan's own territorial waters around its southwestern islands in Okinawa Prefecture. Since then, Japanese strategists have become increasingly concerned that China's expansion of its military power is focussed not just on the prevention of Taiwan's independence, but is now looking to actively take the island back by force and, moreover, is looking to challenge the wider military and territorial status quo in the Asia-Pacific.

China's rapid expansion of defence budgets and military modernisation – manifested in its investment in extensive ballistic and cruise missile programmes, blue water naval capabilities, amphibious capabilities and aircraft carriers, fifth-generation fighters, space and cyber capabilities, as well as unmanned air and undersea vehicles – is seen to lack transparency, but essentially driving at the goal of anti-access area denial (A2/AD) and eventually area control over the first island chain in the East China Sea and South China Sea. China is viewed as transgressing established international norms relating to freedom of navigation and exclusive economic zones (EEZ) and gradually levering out the US military presence and ability to intervene in regional conflicts and in support of its allies. Indeed, Japanese strategists suspect that China is seeking not only to complicate and marginalise US influence, but eventually to be capable of defeating the United States in a full-scale regional conflict and supersede its military hegemony.

Most concerningly for Japan itself, Japanese leaders perceive that China's territorial irredentism, coupled with its significant military modernisation, places Japan on the frontline in any Taiwan contingency, and poses threats to Japan's sea lines of communication (SLOC) in the South China Sea, and even directly to Japan's own control of disputed maritime zones and outlying islands, including the Senkaku/Diaoyu islands, in the East China Sea. The 2010 incident involving a clash between a Japan Coast Guard (JCG) vessel and a Chinese trawler in the East China Sea around the Senkaku Islands that subsequently precipitated a presumed Chinese embargo of rare earth materials to Japan, and a further intensification of the Chinese maritime presence in the region, served as a turning point to confirm to Japanese policymakers that China was not just posturing on territorial issues but had serious intent to acquire territory by force if necessary (Pugliese and Insisa 2017: 47–8; Koga 2018: 647–8).

For Japan, anxieties over China are accentuated by attempting to read US intentions. As Sino-US tensions have increased in recent years, and the offence-defence balance starts to tilt in China's favour, Japan perceives becoming caught in strategic competition between the existing and emerging superpowers. Japan might then face risks of entrapment in any Sino-US conflict over Taiwan or other regional issues, but might also face, even more hazardously, abandonment if the United States does not maintain the military capability or political will to uphold security guarantees (Magosaki 2012: 130–4; Liff 2017: 158). Successive Japanese administrations have, therefore, driven at the United States confirming explicitly that Article 5 of the security treaty extends US defensive obligations over the Senkaku Islands, and successfully gained public assurances from presidents Barack Obama in 2014, Donald J. Trump in 2017, and Biden in 2021.

Finally, in terms of the immediate regional security environment, although Japan has watched with care over the last two decades the reform and modernisation of the Armed Forces of the Russian Federation's conventional and nuclear forces, Russia's invasion of Ukraine in 2022 made apparent the potential renewed threat to Japan itself via the Northern Territories and enhanced Russian military activity around the Japanese archipelago (Bōeishō 2021a: 86–8). At times, and additionally concerning for Japan, Russia's activity has been coordinated with China, as with the passage of a flotilla of ten Russian and

Chinese warships through the Tsugaru Strait between Hokkaidō and Honshū in October 2021.

The recent perceived waxing and waning of US capabilities and commitments to the Asia-Pacific region and its security has been a further complication. The Obama administration's initial perceived flirtation with strategic accommodation with China was viewed as problematic in Tokyo, but its subsequent 'pivot' to Asia offered a degree of reassurance, if with still lingering doubts over the US's deployment of sufficient military deterrent capacity in the region (Green 2017: 523–8). Trump's increasingly tougher line on China in economics, diplomacy, and security again offered some reassurance to Japan, although his administration's unpredictability and transactional approach to its alliance ties did not entirely eliminate concerns of abandonment (Hikotani 2017). The Biden administration, although initially engendering concerns of once again the United States seeking an accommodation with China, has thus far proved a more predictable alliance partner and spoken resolutely in supporting allies on security issues towards China.

In turn, Japan's increasingly fluid international environment has contributed to domestic political change, which has then fed into further changes in thinking through new parameters for strategy and defence. The LDP's previously ineluctable hold on power was shaken by the apparent demise of external threats in the early post–Cold War period that weakened the legitimacy of its anti-communist security stance. The party's general competency to govern was further questioned by Japan's entry into a period of long-term economic malaise and 'lost decades' of perceived national decline. The consequence of the collapse of the '1955 system' has been the LDP's increasing orientation away from the 'mainstream' and the return to influence of internal factions more focussed at times on neoliberal economic remedies and the search for a new legitimacy by espousing Japan's need to restore a sense of national identity and adopt revisionist views on security and issues of history (Harris 2020: 47–58). At the same time, the SDPJ, the former main opposition party, entered into a near terminal decline as the relevance of its anti-militaristic stance was questioned at the conclusion of the Cold War due to reduced fears of Japan's involvement in external conflict, and then by undermining its own legitimacy through entering into an ill-fated coalition in the mid-1990s with its former arch-adversary the LDP that necessitated betraying its long-held position of the JSDF as unconstitutional (Pyle 2018: 361). Meanwhile, the LDP, to shore up its domestic position, entered from 1999 to the present day into a long-running electoral cooperation and coalition arrangement with the Kōmeitō regarded as more dovish on security matters.

The LDP subsequently encountered more serious opposition from the centrist Democratic Party of Japan (DPJ), even losing power to its rival from 2009 to 2012. The result for Japanese politics has been periods of relative stability during the long-running premierships of Koizumi Junichirō (2001–6) and most recently Abe, punctuated by periods of instability as during the five years between 2006 and 2011 when the country was led by six different prime ministers from the LDP and DPJ. In addition, the DPJ itself split and reformed as the Democratic Party (DP) in 2016 and merging with other parties to form the Democratic Party for the People in 2018. In its place, the Constitutional Democratic Party of Japan (CDPJ), itself a splinter group of the DP, has arisen as the main, if smaller opposition party. Abe's fall from power in 2020 may have returned Japan back to a degree of relative instability given Suga's one-year premiership and rapid replacement by Kishida.

But even during political uncertainty there has been convergence on security policy. LDP and DPJ members, although often at loggerheads over the precise direction of Japan's security orientation, have overlapped in advocating for Japan to boost its security efforts overall (Hughes 2012; Catalinac 2016; Liff 2021: 499–500). The CDPJ, whilst continuing to promote constitutional pacifism and an exclusively defence-oriented posture, readily accepts the necessity of the US-Japan alliance. Moreover, the LDP, despite its struggle to recover its past reputation for competence and to gain popular traction with its revisionist ideology, and its reliance in coalition on the Kōmeitō that can on occasion modify LDP policy, has maintained an impressive electoral machine guaranteeing strong National Diet majorities and enabling it to effect its overall military agenda without truly significant domestic opposition (Hughes 2017: 122–6).

2.3 Japan's Reformulation of Grand Strategy and Military Doctrine

As Japan's strategic prospects over the last three decades have become more disrupted, changing international and domestic drivers have pointed to the post-war status quo in the form of the Yoshida Doctrine as increasingly untenable. The essential debate for policymakers has thus become how to conceptualise the future of security threats, the international security order, and where Japan should respond and focus its efforts, and so work towards the adaptation or even rethinking of its grand strategy and military role.

A series of reports by prime ministerial advisory groups on defence and security, and related Japan Ministry of Defence (JMOD) NDPGs, produced under LDP and DPJ governments from the early post–Cold War onwards to the present day, trace the process of Japanese strategic thinking undergoing a fundamental transformation. These documents have all progressively pointed to a range of new security challenges faced by Japan including the proliferation of ballistic missiles and WMD, regional conflicts centred on territorial disputes, North Korea's growing threat, and China's rise. In turn, these documents have argued that these challenges are compounded by the relative decline of US supremacy and shifting balance of power, and as a result Japan can no longer stand aside and be isolated from regional and global security trends (Bōei Mondai Kondankai 1994: 3; Anzen Hoshō to Bōeiryoku ni Kansuru Kondankai 2004: 3–4; Bōeichō 2004; Anzen Hoshō to Bōeiryoku ni Kansuru Kondankai 2009: 6–12, 14–16; Arata na Jidai no Anzen Hoshō to Bōeiryoku ni Kansuru Kondankai 2010: v-vi; JMOD 2010: 2–3).

A watershed moment for revising the assumptions of existing grand strategy then came with the creation of the first NSS in December 2013 under the Abe administration. The NSS repeated the emphasis of previous advisory reports and NDPGs on the challenges posed by certain capabilities and states, and especially China, and that the backdrop to these issues was the shifting global and Asia-Pacific balance of power away from US untrammelled supremacy. The NSS expressed the essential transformation of Japan's security situation, arguing that the advancement of globalisation and technological innovation, changing balance of power in the Asia-Pacific, and rise of China, meant, 'threats, irrespective of where they originate in the world, could instantly have a direct influence on the security of Japan'. Consequently, the NSS asserted that 'Japan cannot secure its own peace and security by itself, and the international community expects Japan to play a more proactive role for peace and stability in the world, in a way commensurate with its national capabilities' (Kokka Anzen Hoshō Kaigi 2013: 3, 5). This new mantra was to penetrate across Japanese official security and military discourse for the next decade onwards.

Abe's Advisory Panel on the Reconstruction for the Legal Basis of Security – first convened from 2006 to 2008, and then reconvened from 2013 to 2014, to examine the case for the exercise of the right of collective self-defence and comprising many of the same strategic thinkers that had contributed to previous prime ministerial advisory reports – confirmed this new Japanese understanding of international security. The panel argued that in the new century many diverse security threats had emerged, exacerbated in reach and impact by advances in military technology, and in large part the result of the shifting balance of power. This meant no nation could any longer defend itself entirely alone and international collective responses were now indispensable. In particular, the report emphasised that the key to Japan's security remained the US-Japan alliance and it was primarily in scenarios of cooperation with the United States that the right of collective self-defence should be exercised (Anzen Hoshō no Hō-teki Kiban no Saikōchiku ni Kansuru Kondankai 2008; Anzen Hoshō no Hō-teki Kiban no Saikōchiku ni Kansuru Kondankai 2014: 10, 13–22).

The shift in Japan's understanding of its international security was epitomised by the pronouncement of the Abe Cabinet regarding its advocacy for the exercise of the right of collective self-defence in May 2014. The statement reiterated that the shift in the global balance of power, rapid progress of technological innovation, and proliferation of WMD and ballistic missiles meant, 'any threats, irrespective of where they originate in the world, could have a direct influence on the security of Japan ... No country can secure its own peace only by itself, and the international community also expects Japan to play a more proactive role for peace and stability in the world, in a way commensurate with its national capability' (Kokka Anzen Hoshō Kaigi Kettei, Kakugi Kettei 2014).

The revisions of the NDPG in 2013 and again in 2018 repeated the Japanese government line that the surrounding security situation under conditions of the relative decline of US influence and 'multi-polarisation' of the international system had become far more complex, presented diverse challenges, and that it was difficult for a single country to deal with alone, so necessitating in response shared and more active international cooperation. Japan's own response to these challenges was again its declared intention to enhance national deterrence efforts, to strengthen the US-Japan alliance for more effective cooperation, and to promote active security cooperation in the Asia-Pacific region (JMOD 2013: 1, 4, 6–13; JMOD 2018: 1–3, 8–17).

2.4 The Abe Doctrine as Grand Strategy and Japan's Multi-Layered Military Approach

In turn, Japan's diagnosis of its fundamentally transformed global and regional security situation has produced a consistent set of thinking around the need to revisit grand strategy and the necessary approaches to share the burden of fending for its security. Prime ministerial advisory reports and NDPGs started to discuss the importance of Japan diversifying its approaches to security. This included in the early post–Cold War period more engagement with multilateral frameworks such as UNPKO and regional security dialogue (Bōei Mondai Kondankai 1994: 10). In addition, a constant theme has been that Japan should not only be capable of defeating threats once they reach its territory but attempt to stop these arising in the first place and to push outwards its security perimeter and responsibilities. The reports have converged on the conclusion that Japan should adopt a more 'integrated' or 'multi-layered cooperative security strategy' that comprises: first,

Japan's own national military policies; second, the US-Japan alliance; and, third, cooperation with other countries in the region and the international community (Anzen Hoshō to Bōeiryoku ni Kansuru Kondankai 2004: 4–5; Bōeichō 2004; Anzen Hoshō to Bōeiryoku ni Kansuru Kondankai 2009: 18–20; Arata na Jidai no Anzen Hoshō to Bōeiryoku ni Kansuru Kondankai 2010: vi; JMOD 2010: 2).

The NSS subsequently adopted a similar position that Japan should strengthen its own defensive capability, in combination with efforts to prevent threats reaching Japan through US-Japan cooperation, cooperation with other partners in the Asia-Pacific, and to improve the global security environment by promoting 'an international order based on universal values and rules, playing a leading role in the settlement of disputes, through consistent diplomatic efforts and further personnel contributions' (Kokka Anzen Hoshō Kaigi 2013: 5–6). The 2013 and 2018 NDPGs then adopted this approach of Japanese efforts for a comprehensive national defence architecture, a strengthened US-Japan alliance, and increased cooperation with a range of regional and global partners (JMOD 2013: 6–13; JMOD 2018).

This gradual but relentless shift in the mindset of Japan's strategists and seeming propensity to 'go global' in terms of geographical scope, missions, and partners, thus culminated in the new security concept propounded by Abe of a 'proactive contribution to peace' (*sekkyoku-teki heiwashugi*) and ensconced in the NSS. Japan's proactive contribution to peace is fleshed out in the NSS in line with the three-fold approach of its own defence, cooperation with the United States, and cooperation with the wider international community. Japan's own defence efforts include a focus on territorial defence, maritime security, cyber security, outer space, intelligence capabilities, and military equipment and technologies. The US-Japan alliance focus is on deepening and broadening areas of defence cooperation and deterrence, and on maintaining the US force presence in Japan. International cooperation is focussed on the Asia-Pacific and on states with which it shares 'universal values' and strategic interests, including Australia, India, South Korea, and ASEAN. Beyond the Asia-Pacific, the NSS fixes on cooperation with European states that share its desire to uphold the existing international order; key states in Latin America, Africa, and the Middle East; tackling international terrorism; strengthening the overall rule of law; and promoting international peace cooperation with the UN.

The NSS and a 'proactive contribution to peace' have subsequently framed much of Japan's diplomatic and security discourse as projected outwards to the international community. Abe consistently roadshowed the concept in the United States, Europe, India, Africa, ASEAN, and Australia, to look for international endorsements. The concept subsequently became the central motif for articulating Japan's diplomacy and economic statecraft and official development assistance

(ODA), and thus not just strictly its security and defence policy (Dobson 2017). Furthermore, the concept was carried over as a central plank of the Suga administration's diplomatic and security policy (MOFA 2020a) and the new Kishida administration has indicated no move away from it in preparing the first NSS revision at the end of 2022. Most crucially, the discourse of a proactive contribution to peace, the associated view that no state including Japan can guarantee security by itself, and the consequent appeal simultaneously to domestic and international audiences of the need for Japan to move along this path, has encapsulated and furthered the arguments of Japanese policymakers in favour of the exercise of collective self-defence, and paved the way for the 2015 security legislation breaching the ban.

Japan's new assessments of its post–Cold War security environment, and acknowledgement that it needs to shift its responses to include enhanced international cooperation and measures such as collective self-defence, have subsequently facilitated a shift in overall grand strategy. For many Japanese policymakers, the Yoshida Doctrine's assumptions and practices are now seen as untenable. Instead, Abe inspired the effective dismantling of the Yoshida Doctrine and the advent of an eponymous 'Abe Doctrine'. This revised grand strategy incorporates the changes noted above in the concept of a proactive contribution to peace, of seeking to move Japan away from a minimalist defence posture and to now upgrade key areas of JSDF capabilities and to remove constitutional constraints on the use of military power for international security (Hanssen 2020: 186–194). Japan under the doctrine should similarly move away from a minimalist level of commitment to US security objectives, cease constant hedging against alliance dilemmas, and function as a more fully-fledged and integrated US-Japan alliance partner. Finally, Japan should look to exercise more overt leadership in East Asia and beyond, refusing to accede to a rising China's dominance in the region, and shifting from default to more conditional engagement and balancing if necessary. Japan should maintain economic ties but diversify from risks of asymmetric dependence on China, and in security deal with its neighbour from a position of strength and adopt incipient hard and soft counterbalancing vis-à-vis its neighbour's military assertiveness (Hughes 2016; Envall 2020; Hughes, Patalano, and Ward 2021).

Japanese ambitions on the back of the proactive contribution to peace and Abe Doctrine have also extended into proposing concepts for the wider regional security order. Abe in 2016 put forward the FOIP concept that sought to emphasise a region that would guarantee international public goods based on the 'rules-based international order', with three central areas of cooperation around free trade, economic development and particularly quality infrastructure, and peace and stability through maritime law enforcement and humanitarian assistance and disaster relief (HADR) (MOFA 2016b, 2020b). Japan has avoided the language of FOIP being directed at any one state and posits an inclusive region, that is ASEAN-centred, connecting the Asia-Pacific through to the Indian Ocean and Africa, and willing to cooperate with any like-minded state inside or outside its geographical scope, even stretching to European states (Satake and Sahashi 2021). Likewise, Japanese policymakers now refer to FOIP as a vision rather than strategy to avoid a sense of containing a particular state (Hosoya 2019a; Michishita 2022). Nevertheless, FOIP, as adopted by the Abe, Suga, and Kishida administrations, is undoubtedly a strategy to curb China's influence in the region and counter the influence of the Belt and Road Initiative (BRI).

2.5 Conclusion

Japan's changed perceptions of its security environment, revised security and grand strategies, and articulation of new concepts for the regional security order, all indicate its military posture is indeed undergoing a fundamental transformation. This shifting stance purports to offer Japan new opportunities for regional and global military cooperation across a range of functions, and that should extend beyond not just the United States but to a range of new partners. The language of the proactive contribution to peace and a multi-layered security policy implies a seemingly new internationalist bent and for Japan to undertake significant military responsibilities that extend beyond its own immediate territorial defence, into the Asia-Pacific and Indo-Pacific regions, and that include deeper cooperation with multilateral frameworks.

However, subsequent sections of this Element explore whether this is an accurate set of expectations for Japan and whether its official rhetoric, or the rhetoric used about it, matches the reality of Japan's military role. Japan's military role has certainly transformed for all the reasons outlined above of policymakers' new strategic threat assessments, and the consequent acceptance of the need to adopt new security concepts and a revised grand strategy, to become more proactive, and to seek out additional security partners beyond the US-Japan alliance. More doubtful, though, is the extent to which Japan has sought the type of internationalist and more broad-based, multi-directional, and fully multi-layered security strategy that has been often ascribed to it in recent years. It is instead the case that Japan's 'proactive contribution to peace' has been very selective in nature, focussed most fully on its own immediate territorial security and shoring up cooperation with the United States to serve bilateral strategic ends. Meanwhile, other forms of cooperation internationally, even if expanding in number, have still been arrayed around these imperatives, demoted in priority, or even largely neglected if felt incompatible with them.

3 Transforming Defence Doctrine and Capabilities

Japan's national comprehensive defence architecture – the first layer of its declared proactive contribution to peace – has undergone significant shifts in terms of doctrines and procurement of capabilities in the last three decades. The JSDF as a result has indeed become a more proactive and capable force, and a potential new partner for cooperation with other militaries. Nevertheless, this new JSDF proactivity and potential for international cooperation still has major limitations, many of which are now less to do with anti-militaristic, legal, or constitutional constraints that have been eroded or abandoned, and instead specific strategic choices despite increased operational flexibility. The JSDF's development of doctrines and capabilities has become increasingly focussed on Japan's own immediate homeland and regional defensive needs and, consequently, cooperation with its US ally, and with other US allies and partners, to achieve these objectives, with broader international security cooperation as a lesser priority.

3.1 From Basic Defence Force to Multi-Domain Defence Force

Japan's defence planners in the post–Cold War period have set about systematically eroding and then discarding constraints on the JSDF's operational capabilities. Much of the principal thrust of these changes has come via successive revisions of the NDPG and Mid-Term Defence Programme (MTDP). Japan in the post-war period has adopted an 'exclusively defence-oriented policy' and this stance was consolidated in the 1976 NDPG and the JSDF's Basic Defence Force (BDF) concept (*kiban-teki bōeiryoku*). The BDF stressed that the JSDF would maintain a force structure to enable it by itself to repel limited direct aggression, but that in cases where this aggression proved too great it would employ a force structure capable of effective resistance until US cooperation could be introduced. Consequently, the BDF made for an essentially static JSDF defence posture, with heavy GSDF forces and supporting MSDF and ASDF assets oriented towards denying a full-scale Soviet invasion of the main Japanese archipelago. In the post–Cold War period, the first revised 1995 NDPG and then the 2004 NDPG began to chip away at the BDF doctrine, stating respectively that the JSDF in the event of any form of direct aggression would now seek from the outset to repel this with US assistance, and that it would develop the ability to work proactively to contribute to international peace cooperation activities and respond to new threats and contingencies – so starting to converge Japanese and US defence postures, and indicating a new intent to enhance JSDF regional and global mobility (Bōeichō 2004).

In line with the plans for a multi-layered security strategy, ensuing NDPG revisions have sought to transform JSDF doctrine and capabilities to respond to Asia-Pacific and global security exigencies through pledging enhanced cooperation with regional bilateral and multilateral partners and robust international peace cooperation activities. Inevitably, though, the NDPGs have devoted the strongest emphasis to Japan's homeland defence needs. Recognising China's rise and North Korea's adventurism, NDPG revisions have stressed JSDF responses to renewed concerns of ensuring the security of the sea and air space surrounding Japan, deterring attacks on offshore islands, and preventing ballistic missile attacks. Revisions of the NDPG have also drawn constant attention to 'grey-zone' situations in the Asia-Pacific region, defined as confrontations over territory, sovereignty, and economic interests that sit in the indistinct zone between pure peacetime and a military contingency. These types of situations, envisaged to encompass principally China's maritime incursions around Japan's offshore islands, are felt to be especially hazardous, given that these could escalate into attempts by Chinese civilian or paramilitary forces to seize the islands as a *fait accompli*, but posing questions for the JSDF as to whether it has the mandate to respond with force and whether US-Japan treaty obligations might cover such situations.

The 2010 NDPG then formally cast-off the BDF and the last vestiges of Cold War planning, adopting instead a new concept of the Dynamic Defence Force (DDF) (*dō-teki bōeiryoku*) (JMOD 2010). The DDF to meet multiple security challenges was to be characterised by 'readiness, mobility, flexibility, sustainability, and versatility', undergirded by advanced technology and intelligence capabilities. In turn, the JSDF was not only to undertake a more active posture in and around Japanese territory, but also started to shift many of its deployments southwards to meet new challenges emanating from China in terms of territorial disputes and maritime security in the East China Sea (Katagiri 2020: 187). The 2013 NDPG further advanced JSDF doctrinal change by upgrading the DDF to a Joint Dynamic Defence Force (JDDF) (*tōgō kidō bōeiryoku*) to enable the GSDF, MSDF, and ASDF to work more effectively in joint fashion (JMOD 2013). The 2018 NDPG went a step further with the ambition to transform the JSDF services in combination into a Multi-Domain Defence Force (MDDF) (*tajigen tōgō bōeiryoku*) to engage in 'cross-domain operations' (*ryōiki ōdan sakusen*), not only across the land, sea, and air domains, but now also across outer space, cyberspace, and electronic warfare (JMOD 2018).

3.2 GSDF

The GSDF during the Cold War represented the apotheosis of Japan's essentially static deployment and denial strategy with heavy concentrations of MBTs and long-range artillery in Hokkaidō to ward off Soviet incursions. The GSDF was divided into five regional armies that lacked a centralised operational command, so hampering the movement of personnel, logistics, and weapons amongst the armies that remained focussed on their localised area of defence (Hornung 2020: 22). In the immediate post–Cold War period, as outlined in Section 1, the GSDF started to shift its posture given the emergence of new overseas despatch roles in military operations other than war, including: UNPKO reconstruction activities, with the largest-scale deployments in Cambodia (1992–3), East Timor and Timor-Leste (2002–3) and South Sudan (2011–17); HADR missions in the Asia-Pacific and beyond; US-led coalition reconstruction support activities in Iraq (2004–6); and domestic natural disaster responses and most notably the Great East Japan Earthquake in 2011 (Samuels 2013: 80–109).

The 1995 NDPG and successive NDPGs, acknowledging the need to move away from the immobile Cold War defence posture, started a long-term process of building-down the GSDF's MBT and artillery numbers (Table 1); and the 2004 NDPG mandated the creation in 2007 of a Central Readiness Force (CRF) that combined a Special Forces Group, the 1st Airborne Brigade, 1st Helicopter Brigade, and the 101st NBC (Nuclear, Biological, and Chemical) Protection Unit, and was designed to function as a rapid-reaction force for coordinating nationwide mobile operations, responses to domestic terrorism, guerrilla incursions and NBC warfare, and training personnel for overseas deployment (Heginbotham and Samuels 2018: 143–4).

The GSDF, pursuant to the NDPGs and MTDPs from 2010 onwards, shifted its posture even more firmly, continuing with the trends towards mobility and jointness, but now with a declining focus on overseas despatch and very much returning to homeland defence, and especially the defence of Japan's southwestern islands. The principal effort of the GSDF has been to establish garrisons and coastal observation units (COU) on the islands of Yonaguni (160 personnel), Amami-Ōshima (550 personnel), Miyako (700–800 personnel), and Ishigaki (500–600 personnel), tasked with monitoring Chinese activities and potentially jamming communications, and with the latter three locations hosting deployments of surface-to-air missile (SAM) batteries and anti-ship cruise missile (ASCM) batteries. The GSDF for the first time also announced its intention in September 2021 to deploy surface-to-surface missiles (SSM) on the main island of Okinawa by 2023. The GSDF has also devoted considerable efforts not only to defending these islands, but also for the possibility of retaking the islands if seized by an aggressor. The ARDB stood up in March 2018 as a 'proto-marine corps', is planned to reach a total strength of 3,000 personnel, and

Table 1 Comparison of NDPGs from 1976 to 2018

		1976 NDPG	1995 NDPG	2004 NDPG	2010 NDPG	2013 NDPG	2018 NDPG
	GSDF personnel	180,000	160,000	155,000	154,000	159,000	159,000
	Regular personnel		145,000	148,000	147,000	151,000	151,000
	Ready reserve personnel		15,000	7,000	7,000	8,000	8,000
GSDF							
	Main equipment						
	Battle tanks	approx. 1,200	approx. 900	approx. 600	approx. 400	approx. 560	approx. 560
	Artillery	approx. 1,000	approx. 900	approx. 600	approx. 400	approx. 400	approx. 400
MSDF	**Main equipment**						
	Destroyers	approx. 60	approx. 50	47	48	54	54
	Submarines	16	16	16	22	22	22
	Combat aircraft	approx. 220	approx. 170	approx. 150	approx. 150	approx. 170	approx. 190
ASDF	**Main equipment**						
	Combat aircraft	approx. 400	approx. 400	approx. 350	approx. 340	approx. 360	approx. 370
	Fighters (included in combat aircraft)	approx. 350	approx. 300	approx. 260	approx. 260	approx. 280	approx. 290

Source: Boeishō, *Bōei Hakusho*. Tokyo: Ōkurashō Insatsukyoku, various years.

consists of two amphibious regiments, one amphibious assault battalion, one field artillery battalion, one reconnaissance company, a signal company, an engineer company, and a logistics support battalion (Hornung 2020: 24).

More generally, the GSDF has sought to enhance its overall mobility by reorganising half of its operational units into rapid deployment divisions and brigades able to carry out nation-wide strategic manoeuvre and capable of transport by air. The GSDF has also moved to centralise its command functions by creating in March 2018 the Ground Component Command (GCC) that has operational control over regional army units and has also taken over the command of the ARDB and the units previously under the now disestablished CRF (Hornung 2020: 22, 23–4).

To support these roles and force structures, the GSDF has invested in the procurement of the necessary capabilities for enhanced mobility in and around the Japanese archipelago. The GSDF has procured Type 96 Wheeled Armoured Personnel Carriers (with an improved variant due also for procurement) and Type 16 Manoeuvre Combat Vehicles, for deployment in UNPKOs overseas, but also suitable for island defence, and transportable by air. The ARDB is procuring 52 of the United States's Amphibious Assault Vehicle-7s (AAV-7) to provide for its amphibious capability. The GSDF, even whilst reducing total tank numbers, has continued to invest in advanced MBTs in the shape of the Type 90 and its new replacement the Type 10 designed to be lighter to suit terrain and transport routes across Japan. The GSDF deploys AH-1 *Cobra* and AH-64 *Apache* for its attack helicopters. For air transport, the GSDF has long deployed the fixed-rotor CH-47JA and has started to procure 17 tilt-rotor V-22 *Ospreys* from the United States. The GSDF was also reported in 2021 as seeking to acquire by 2024 one medium-sized (2,000 tons) and two small-sized transports (400 tons) for the supply of troops on the southwestern islands, marking for the first time the GSDF's procurement of its own ships (*Japan Times* 2021a). The GSDF's increasing focus on island defence is also represented in its investment in and deployment of missile capabilities. The Type 03 SAM with a 50-kilometre range deployed on three of the southwestern islands offers strong air defence and is likely to be replaced with an upgraded 100-kilometre range Type 03 capable of tracking multiple targets simultaneously. The Type 12 ASCM with a 200-kilometre range provides the capability for the GSDF to engage ships from a considerable distance and to, in effect, close off the sea passages to any aggressor around the southwestern islands and between these islands and Taiwan.

3.3 MSDF

The MSDF, for its part, has long contrasted with the GSDF regarding the diversity and international outlook of its roles and capabilities. Nevertheless, the MSDF, despite expanding its international engagement significantly during and after the Cold War, has in most recent years, not unlike the GSDF, also retrenched in focussing on the immediate defence of Japan itself. During the early Cold War period, the MSDF was charged with the principal missions of 'sea denial' and 'choke point' control of the immediate waters and key straits around Japan to assist in preventing a Soviet land invasion from the sea and the breakout of the Soviet Navy into the Western Pacific. Although the MSDF did not work jointly with the GSDF it still performed a complementary role in the BDF and invasion denial strategy. As the Cold War progressed, the MSDF acquired an expanded role in support of the US Navy (USN). The 1978 Guidelines for US-Japan Defense Cooperation made clear that the MSDF was charged not only primarily with the defence of Japanese sea space, leaving the United States unencumbered from defensive duties to deploy strike power in the East Asia region, but should also undertake SLOC defence. Prime Minister Suzuki Zenkō during a visit to Washington DC in 1981 subsequently pledged that the MSDF would defend SLOCs up to 1,000 nautical miles beyond Japan's immediate territorial waters.

The MSDF in this period thus established a role that as a naval force was inherently mobile and expanding geographically in reach. Its role was also highly complementary and coordinated with the United States and involved direct bilateral navy-to-navy cooperation. The USN's fostering of the MSDF participation in bilateral exercises within the multilateral Rim of the Pacific (RIMPAC) exercises from 1980 onwards also meant the MSDF started to observe cooperation amongst other international navies. The MSDF was as a result positioned at the forefront of the emerging 'shield' and 'spear' military division of labour between Japan and the US, and its procurement of capabilities was increasingly geared to serve this relationship. The MSDF built up a significant force of destroyers, P-3C patrol aircraft, and submarines to defend Japan, bottle up the Soviet fleet, and free up the USN for offensive power projection.

In the post–Cold War period, the MSDF has continued to expand the geographical extent of its deployments, range of missions, and international partners, so providing it with the greatest potential for a more proactive Japanese international security role. The MSDF's role in these activities is considered in more detail in Sections 4 and 5, and has comprised the original 1991 Persian Gulf minesweeping despatch; non-combat refuelling operations for coalition ships engaged in Operation Enduring Freedom (OEF) in the Indian Ocean from 2002 to 2009; despatch in 2004 to support GSDF deployments on non-combat reconstruction missions in Iraq as part of Operation Iraqi Freedom; and engagement in counter-piracy missions off the coast of

Somalia and in the Gulf of Aden from 2009 onwards. The MSDF has also performed important HADR missions in Indonesia from 2004–5 and the Philippines in 2013.

At the same time as acquiring these additional missions, however, and not dissimilar from the GSDF's experience, the MSDF's encountering of threats from North Korea and the relentless rise of China has meant that the adoption of a broader international security role has been constrained and received less priority than the once again overriding need to respond to the defence of the Japanese homeland and immediate East Asia region, and related US-Japan alliance demands. The successive revisions of the NDPG and MTDP chart the shift of the MSDF's role from broadening to then limiting horizons over the past three decades

The 1995 NDPG, as with the other JSDF services, started to downsize the MSDF's Cold War-oriented force structure, seeking to reduce the number of destroyers and patrol aircraft to release resources to modernise the destroyer fleet and introduce new *Oyashio*-class submarines and a design for a new P-1 patrol aircraft – all designed to respond to North Korea and the looming rise of China (Table 1). The MSDF further commissioned three *Ōsumi*-class landing ships between 1993 and 1999 for the support of nascent amphibious operations and deployment of landing craft (Hinata-Yamaguchi 2018). The flat tops of the vessels also enable deployment of up to two CH-47 transport helicopters and have demonstrated the ability to land United States Marines Corps (USMC) V-22 *Ospreys*. The MSDF more recently refitted these vessels to deploy the GSDF ARDB's AAVs.

In the 2004 NDPG, the MSDF retained its key role of controlling the surrounding sea space but was to move away from the Cold War-style near-exclusive emphasis on ASW, and to diversify its missions in support of the other JSDF services. Most importantly, BMD was designated as a core mission for the MSDF and thus a large proportion of its destroyer fleet and capabilities – whilst multifunctional for BMD and other missions in other regions – was oriented towards the direct defence of Japanese land territory. The MTDP reduced the overall number of the MSDF's destroyers to 47, in part due to Japan's tightening defence budget constraints, but also to make room for continuing procurements of *Atago*-class *Aegis* destroyers, SH-60K patrol helicopters, MCH-101 mine-sweeper helicopters, and the new P-1 patrol aircraft (Bōeichō 2004: 3–4). The MSDF also introduced the new 13,500-tonne *Hyūga*-class DDHs, in essence light helicopter carriers, with a primary role for ASW but also able to serve as platforms for command-and-control of amphibious operations and helicopter support for GSDF amphibious operations to retake offshore islands.

The 2010 NDPG and its abandonment of the BDF concept in favour of the DDF further prioritised MSDF missions in defending Japan's immediate territory. The destroyer fleet was again to increase to 48 and the submarine fleet to 22 (JMOD 2010). The 2013 NDPG's adoption of the JDDF confirmed the MSDF's roles in defending the surrounding sea space and offshore islands in joint cooperation with the other JSDF services, and the importance of US-Japan cooperation in BMD and supporting the United States to mount interventions across the first and second island chains (JMOD 2013: 22–3; Patalano 2014: 417–19). The MTDP boosted MSDF destroyer numbers to 54 and maintained submarine numbers at 22. The build-up continued of *Aegis* destroyers, P-1s and helicopters, and designs were introduced for a new *Mogami*-class destroyer with compact hulls and designated as future multi-mission frigate (JMOD 2013: 5–8). The *Mogami*-class design appears inspired by the United States's littoral combat ships, with hull stealth technology, anti-ship missiles, vertical launch systems (VLS), and the ability to deploy unmanned underwater vehicles (UUV) and unmanned surface vehicles (USV), and hence a strong emphasis on operating close to shore and to counter A2/AD threats and included as part of the JMOD's efforts for offshore island defence (Boeishō 2021b: 223).

The 2018 NDPG's shift to the MDDF and the focus on JSDF joint operations again highlighted the pivotal role of the MSDF in controlling the surrounding sea space for homeland defence. The MSDF in the MTDP maintained its 54 destroyers and 22 submarines and was to boost its aircraft numbers from 170 to 190. The MSDF introduced a new *Maya*-class *Aegis* destroyer, equipped with Cooperative Engagement Capability (CEC) and Engagement on Remote (EOR) to enable the sharing of targeting and missile guidance information with MSDF aircraft, ASDF aircraft, and USN vessels. The *Taigei*-class submarine has also been commissioned with a new combat management system, lithium-ion batteries to extend its range, and capable of deploying the UGM-84 L Harpoon Block II 250-kilometre anti-ship and land-strike missile. The MSDF for intelligence, surveillance, and reconnaissance (ISR) was to introduce UUVs and UAVs, and most strikingly was finally given assent to convert its *Izumo*-class DDHs into 'defensive' aircraft carriers to operate ASDF short vertical take-off and landing maritime F-35Bs to provide air defence for offshore island operations, and to network its capabilities with those of the GSDF and ASDF for territorial defence. The MSDF was thus to consolidate its role in territorial defence alongside the other services whilst also acquiring its first fixed-wing aircraft carriers in the post-war period and new power projection (JMOD 2018: 21, 28).

The MSDF was also further set to invest in BMD through its decision in December 2017 to procure two *Aegis Ashore* batteries from the United States for deployment by 2025 and location in the north of Japan in Akita Prefecture and in the south in Yamaguchi Prefecture. *Aegis Ashore* was a potentially attractive option to reinforce the MSDF's upper-tier BMD system: the two batteries providing coverage of the entire Japanese archipelago, and a stable land-based platform for all-weather, year-round defence that could reduce the need for the MSDF's *Aegis* destroyers to be on constant station and the fatiguing of equipment and crews. *Aegis Ashore* was also likely to be operated in part by the GSDF and so further reducing MSDF personnel commitments. The project, however, was eventually cancelled in June 2020 due to issues of local opposition over safety issues, technical feasibility, and spiralling costs from an original US$2.5 billion to an estimated US$6 billion. The JMOD decided to fill the capability left by *Aegis Ashore* through the construction of a further two MSDF *Aegis*-equipped ships.

The MSDF has thus developed in the post–Cold War period into a force increasingly able to project power beyond Japan's own immediate territory and into the East Asia region and beyond. The platforms of the MSDF are multi-functional and capable of cooperating with the other JSDF services and a range of international navies. But it is evident also that over the last decade at least the MSDF has been obliged to concentrate increasingly on the threats from North Korea and China and territorial defence. Moreover, as seen in this section and explored more in Section 4, many of the MSDF's roles and capabilities remain very much oriented towards a shield function to support the spear function of the United States in the bilateral alliance division of labour.

3.4 ASDF

The ASDF for much of the Cold War, as with the GSDF, was focussed exclusively on Japanese territorial defence. In line with the BDF and the overall JSDF strategy of preventing a Soviet invasion, the ASDF's primary missions were defensive counter-air (DCA) to protect Japanese airspace from incursions by the Soviet air forces, and a degree of ground attack and defence of surrounding sea lanes to support the GSDF and MSDF in their missions, even if in complementary rather than joint fashion. The ASDF also assumed, as the Cold War progressed, in the same way as the MSDF, a complementary and crucial role in providing a shield for the USAF and other US forces to operate unfettered from Japan to project offensive power. The ASDF's role in Japanese territorial defence was reflected in its aircraft procurements, with the build-up of large numbers of F-4J and F-15J interceptors, F-1s for ground attack and anti-ship operations, and E-2C Hawkeyes for airborne early warning (AEW) and ISR, and the E-767 Airborne Warning And Control System (AWACS). The ASDF's fighters in this period, to reinforce the exclusively defence-oriented policy and scotch any suspicion of offensive power, were denied the procurement of in-flight refuelling capabilities (Nishikawa 2008: 161–3).

The ASDF by the end of the Cold War was a highly advanced and capable force that had achieved air superiority around the Japanese archipelago and was largely unchallenged by regional rivals. Hence, as with the other JSDF services in the immediate post–Cold War period, the ASDF had increased leeway to expand its international security role, utilising its C-1 transports to support GSDF and MSDF UNPKO, deployments in Iraq, counter-piracy missions, and HADR. The ASDF also developed its new C-2 transport with a longer range and greater payload very much with PKO and HADR missions in mind (Hornung 2020: 42). But again, as with the rest of the JSDF, the ASDF in the last two decades has been pulled back to refocus on Japan's own territorial defence and shield functions in support of the United States.

The modernisation of China's airpower has progressively eroded the ASDF's previous dominance in the region, and the emergence of North Korea's missile capabilities has added the new mission of BMD to the ASDF's portfolio. The 1995 NDPG and MTDP recognised these trends, seeking to reduce the size of the Cold War inventory of fighters from 350 to 300, and to emphasise instead qualitative improvements, including procurement of the F-2 multi-role fighter (Table 1). The 2001–5 MTDP shifted the ASDF posture further with the procurement for the first time of KC-767Js for in-flight refuelling. The ASDF initially justified the procurement as necessary to prolong the time that its fighters can remain airborne and make more efficient use of pilot time in the air and fuel for take-off and landing, and to extend the range of its transports engaged in UNPKO and other international cooperation missions (Bōeichō 2002). The 2004 NDPG, recognising the rising concerns over the defence of remote islands, started to move its assets southwards, with the relocation of one F-4J fighter unit from Hyakuri Air Base in Ibaraki Prefecture, north of Tokyo, to Naha Air Base in Okinawa Prefecture. The ASDF also started to deploy from 2007 the Patriot Advanced Capability-3 (PAC-3) for terminal phase BMD. The 2010 NDPG moved an additional squadron of F-15Js and E-2C aircraft to Naha. The ASDF was provided with budget in the 2011–16 MTDP to acquire Joint Direct Attack Munitions (JDAM) for F-2s, in effect precision-guided weapons to replace less sophisticated cluster bombs (Hughes 2009: 42).

The next most significant procurement by the ASDF was the decision in 2011 to replace aging F-4Js with the US F-35A, with initial units of a planned total tranche of 42 units first funded under the 2011–16 and 2014–19 MTDPs. Japan announced in May 2019 that it would procure for the ASDF an extra 63 F-35As under the 2019–23 MTDP, and for the first time 42 F-35Bs for use on MSDF *Izumo*-class DDHs. The ASDF's eventual inventory of 147 F-35s will make it the largest in the world outside the United States itself. The ASDF originally hoped to procure the United States's F-22 *Raptor* to replace the F-4J but was denied this capability due to the United States's refusal to allow any export of this fighter's highly sensitive technology. Japan considered BAE Systems's *Typhoon/ Eurofighter* as an option, which would have offered the opportunity for greater technology transfer to Japan and likely full licenced domestic production. Japan in the end selected the F-35A as the most advanced fifth-generation fighter available, although Japanese defence contractors only have limited opportunities for Final Assembly and Checkout (FACO), and development of elements of the fighter's engine parts, radar, and electro-optical distributed aperture systems rather than building the full aircraft (Hughes 2018: 9).

Japan then went a step further in its 2019–24 MTDP procurements for the ASDF with the decision to equip F-35s with the 500–kilometre range Joint Strike Missile (JSM), and F-15Js with 1,000–kilometre range Joint Air-to-Surface Standoff Missile-Extended Range (JASSM-ER) and the Long-Range Anti-Ship Missile (LRASM). In 2021, the JMOD announced that it would no longer purchase the LRASM from the United States due to rising costs and instead consider the development of a Japanese-made version for F-2 fighters. Japan terms these missiles as a 'stand-off defence capability', although they are in effect cruise missiles. The MTDP further stated that Japan would proceed with research and development into HVGP and hypersonic weapons.

The ASDF is reinforcing its ISR capabilities with the procurement under the 2014–19 and 2019–23 MTDPs of three US-produced RQ-4B *Global Hawk* UAVs that lack an attack capability, and the upgrading of its E-2Cs to E-2Ds that offer greater interoperability with F-35s and possibly CEC in addition. Ground-based sensors have been improved through the upgrading of its fixed-position (FPS) radar sites, including those located on the southwestern islands. The JMOD is further looking to develop indigenously, although with overseas cooperation on key components, an eventual sixth-generation F-X/F-3 replacement for the F-15Js. The F-3 appears to be a large twin-engine air superiority stealth fighter with a superior payload and range to the F-22, and capable of working in tandem with UAVs for ISR and targeting and attack (Bōeishō 2020).

The ASDF, to further integrate and enhance these capabilities, upgraded its existing Base Air Defence Ground Environment (BADGE) to create from 2009 the Japan Aerospace Defence Ground Environment (JADGE). This serves as a command, control, battle management, and communications (C2BMC) system, improving the exchange of information not just for the ASDF but also serving as the command-and-control platform to join up the MSDF's Maritime Operation Force System (MOF), and the GSDF's Division Integrated Communications System (DICS) (Bōeishō 2020: 256, 48, 63).

All these procurements add up to significant new firepower for the ASDF and a doubling down on the mission of assisting defence of the Japanese homeland.

The acquisition of JDAMs and stand-off missiles enables the ASDF to support the GSDF in countering land and sea forces attempting to seize remote islands. The F-35, in combination with these and other recently acquired assets, is a potential game changer in the ASDF's role. The F-35 is not a true interceptor or air superiority fighter like the F-22 and *Eurofighter*, and thus not a straight replacement for the F-4J. However, the F-35, with strong air-to-air combat capabilities, stealth properties, and advanced ISR, electronic warfare and sensor networks, still offers the ASDF a very significant upgrade in its capabilities. The F-35 is able, for instance, to utilise stealth to penetrate air defences and pass real-time information to guide other air assets such as F-2s and F-15Js and their stand-off missiles to their targets. The F-35 also points to the possible switch of long-term strategy from DCA to now offensive counter-air (OCA), with the ASDF's deployment of in-flight refuelling capability, F-35 stealth, and long-range cruise missiles providing the capability to strike at enemy positions inside their own territory to prevent aggression originating against the Japanese homeland. Moreover, as will be elaborated in Sections 3.7 and 4, the F-35, as an 'alliance aircraft', employed by a range of US allies and partners, offers enhanced interoperability with US forces to further buttress the ASDF's shield functions, but also to potentially allow Japan to supplement some traditional spear functions of the United States.

3.5 Space, Cyber, and Electromagnetic Warfare

The MDDF makes explicit the JSDF's core role and capabilities are now to stretch into space, cyber, and electromagnetic warfare (Grønning 2018). Japanese defence planners started to erode the anti-militaristic principle of the 1967 peaceful purposes resolution and to pursue the militarisation of space in reaction to North Korea's Taepdong-1 missile launch over Japanese 'airspace' in 1998. Japan determined that it required an indigenous information-gathering satellite (IGS) constellation utilising optical and radar technologies. The Japanese government to justify their introduction termed the IGSs 'multipurpose' satellites with dual-use civilian functions but the satellites were in effect military spy satellites. The National Diet in 2008 then passed a Basic Space Law that overturned the anti-militaristic principle on the military use of space by stating Japan should limit its usage of space to 'defensive' rather than non-military activities. Successive versions of Japan's Basic Space Plan since 2009 have openly accepted the need for the military use of space. The NSS noted the essential connection between space and national security (Kokka Anzen Hoshō Kaigi 2013). The 2018 NDPG subsequently positioned space as key to supporting cross-domain operations (JMOD 2018).

Japan has moved to militarise space through a series of low-profile but impressive programmes, often in the past obfuscating their military purpose through the 'dual-use' nature of civilian space technology. Japan has developed an indigenous civilian space launch capability, starting in the mid-1980s with the H-II liquid-fuelled rocket series, but since the 1990s extending to the M-series and *Epsilon* solid-fuelled rockets for 'scientific' launches. Solid-fuelled rockets are rarely developed for civilian purposes and the *Epsilon* is considered as a mobile launch-on-demand rocket for military payloads such as tactical satellites (Pekkanen 2020: 27–9). Japan has augmented its satellite capabilities with the Quasi-Zenith Satellite System (QZSS) for positioning, navigation, and timing (PNT) that can support military targeting in the same way as the United States's Global Positioning System (GPS). Japan has further developed satellite capabilities for a variety of functions, including military communications across the JSDF and most notably an X-band satellite network to cover wide maritime expanses around the southwestern islands; signal and electronic intelligence; maritime domain awareness (MDA) around Japan's territorial waters; and space situational awareness (SSA) (Kallender and Hughes 2019). The ASDF in May 2020 established a Space Operations Force to track threats to Japanese surveillance satellites, such as space debris and anti-satellite weapons (ASAT), and in November 2021 established a second unit to monitor electromagnetic threats to its satellites.

The Japanese defence establishment came comparatively late to cyber as a domain of military action, with the JMOD's *Defense of Japan* white papers containing no references to cybersecurity until 2010, and only one brief mention of cybersecurity in the 2004 NDPG (Bōeishō 2010; Bōeichō 2004: 8–9). But the emergence of a series of high-profile breaches in Japan's information security structures – including 2011 attacks on Mitsubishi Heavy Industries (MHI), Japan's largest defence contractor, and its computer systems relating to the design and manufacture of BMD interceptor missiles, fighter planes, and space launch – acted as the necessary shocks to focus attention on Japan's vulnerabilities. That many of these attacks are believed to have originated from China, Russia, and North Korea added impetus for Japan to militarise the cyber domain.

The 2010 and 2013 NDPGs indicated that Japan's objective should be to ensure the 'stable use of cyberspace', and the 2013 NSS similarly identified threats in cyberspace as major risks to the 'global commons' (JMOD 2010: 2, 5; JMOD 2013: 2; Kokka Anzen Hoshō Kaigi 2013: 7–8). The 2011 MTDP called for the JMOD to establish a cyber-defence doctrine and to create a new organisation in the form of the Cyber Defence Group (CDG) to become the core responder to cyberattacks and protect the JSDF's key information network in the shape of the Defence Information Infrastructure (DII). The aim was thus to overcome the previous stove-piping whereby each service, including the GSDF System Protect Unit, the MSDF Communications Security Group, and the

ASDF Computer Security Evaluation Unit, had defended their own systems separately (Kallender and Hughes 2017: 131). The 2018 NDPG mandated the CDG to grow to 300 members by 2023 and is expected to possibly grow to 1,000 in strength (Hornung 2020: 71). Most significantly, the JSDF was tasked with not only defending against cyberattacks but to possess the 'capability to disrupt, during attack against Japan, an opponent's use of cyberspace for the attack', so hinting that it should now develop an active defence or counterattack doctrine for cyber defence (JMOD 2018: 20; Bartlett 2022).

Japan has accelerated its defence efforts in the cyber domain and is undertaking a similar catch-up effort in electromagnetic warfare. The JSDF has invested to date mainly in electronic warfare support for more passive recognition of electromagnetic threats. The JSDF has, though, started to build-up its electronic attack capabilities, with the 2018 NDPG stating that the JSDF, in similar fashion to the cyber domain, should deploy capabilities to neutralise radar and communications of any opponent that seeks to invade Japan (JMOD 2018: 20–1). The JSDF has budgeted since 2019 for the establishment of an Electromagnetic Spectrum Policy Office in the JMOD's Bureau of Defence Buildup Planning and an Electromagnetic Spectrum Domain Planning Section in the Joint Staff. The ASDF has procured the F-35A and F-35B with strong electronic warfare capabilities and is upgrading the F-15J's electronic warfare capabilities. The GSDF is developing a road-mobile Network Electronic Warfare System (NEWS) for electronic reconnaissance and to degrade the command, control, and communications of adversaries; and the JMOD is developing ground-based jamming systems to target enemy airborne early-warning control aircraft and satellites (Bōeishō 2021a: 248; Hornung 2020: 75).

3.6 Defence Expenditure

Japan, for the JSDF to pursue a more proactive and joint military role, clearly needs to provide adequate budgetary resources for this structural transformation. Prime Minister Miki Takeo in 1976 established the principle that defence expenditure should be limited to 1 per cent of GDP, and this has been touted in Japan as another key anti-militaristic principle. Nakasone's administration overtly breached the prohibition in the mid-1980s by pushing defence spending above 1 per cent for several years. Moreover, if Japan's defence budget is calculated on a NATO basis by including pension payments to service personnel (and the NATO methodology being the basis on which Japan chooses to compare its expenditure with other states), then it has always exceeded 1 per cent of GDP (Hughes 2009: 39). However, in the first two decades of the post–Cold War period, after an initial rise to record levels, Japan's defence expenditure plateaued at around ¥5 trillion (nominally US$40–$45 billion), and then started to fall slightly to around ¥4.6 trillion, all whilst remaining around 1 per cent of GDP (Hughes 2019).

Japan's economic downturn since the early 1990s and heavy government debt constrained the expansion of defence spending. Japan has started over the last decade to reverse these trends, though, with the Abe administration implementing annual defence budget increases of 1 to 2 per cent from 2013 to 2020. Abe also indicated in the National Diet in March 2017 that his administration had no necessary intention of suppressing defence expenditure below 1 per cent of GDP and that no such budgetary policy constraint existed, in essence abandoning the previous anti-militaristic constraint. Indeed, the JMOD under the Abe administration achieved the largest defence budgets in the post-war period and firmly back above the ¥5.1 trillion level (Bōeishō 2021a: 191). The Suga administration continued this trend, with the JMOD requesting a record budget of nearly ¥5.5 trillion for fiscal 2022, which was confirmed by the new Kishida Cabinet, and exceeded 1 per cent of GDP (Bōeishō 2021b: 2–3). The LDP's manifesto under Kishida for the 2021 Lower House elections pledged to raise defence expenditure to 2 per cent of GDP (Jiyū Minshutō 2021: 61), and the manifesto for 2022 Upper House elections stated that Japan, taking into consideration the NATO target of 2 per cent of GDP for defence spending, would seek within five years the necessary budget levels to 'radically strengthen' Japan's defence power (Jiyū Minshutō 2022: 116) (Figure).

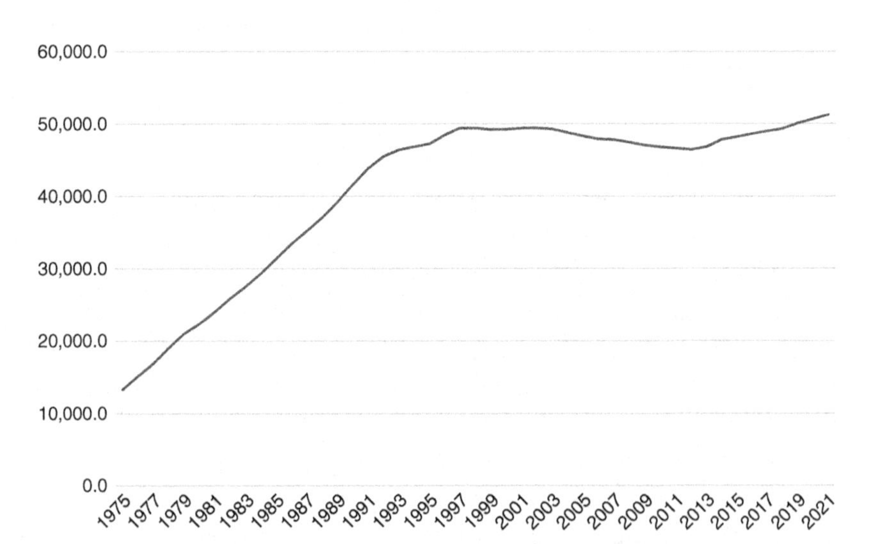

Figure: Japan's defence expenditure 1975–2021 (¥100 million)

Source: Boeishō, *Bōei Hakusho* (Tokyo: Ōkurashō Insatsukyoku), various years.

3.7 Japan's 'Strike' Option?

The JSDF procurement of standoff weapons has stimulated again a Japanese debate on the possession of an 'enemy base attack capability' (*teki kichi kōgeki nōryoku*), or essentially its own strike deterrent capability. The Japanese government has maintained the formal position since 1956 that in the event 'sudden and unjust harm' is inflicted upon Japan by means of a guided missile, then in line with the purport of the constitution that does not mandate passivity in the face of destruction, and within the boundaries of an 'exclusively defence-oriented' policy and using the minimum force possible, it is permitted to launch a strike on enemy missile bases (Asagumo Shimbunsha 2019: 687). Policymakers thereafter did not pursue a strike doctrine or capability, content to rely on US offensive capabilities for strike deterrence against any aggressors.

After the Cold War, however, as North Korea's ballistic missile programmes have advanced and China is seen to pose a threat to Japan's southwestern islands, and as the United States's military dominance is felt to be under increasing challenge, Japanese defence planners have periodically debated the necessity and feasibility of a JSDF strike option (Schoff and Song 2017). Although Japan's principal response to ballistic missile threats has been to invest extensively in BMD and deterrence by denial, it has also become increasingly apparent that these systems may not be sufficient to persuade adversaries to desist from attacks, especially if missiles are used against Japan in large-scale and continuous attacks that saturate its defences (Murano 2020a; Hornung 2020: 78). Japan's concerns over its own capabilities to denude and neutralise missile attacks purely through BMD have been compounded since the decision in 2020 to abandon procurement of *Aegis Ashore* that might have upgraded its defensive capabilities. Moreover, Japanese defence planners are aware that China's A2/AD forces, in being able increasingly to impede, stress, and overburden US offensive capabilities, may call into question its spear functions to support Japan's BMD shield (Iida 2021; Klinger 2021: 9). This issue of such constraints on US offensive capabilities could be particularly acute in the case of attacks on Japan's southwestern islands. If the US military is preoccupied with other larger strategic objectives in a regional contingency, and, given that the southwestern islands are deemed primarily as a Japanese defensive responsibility, the United States may be less willing and able to devote stretched resources and to escalate its use of deterrent capabilities to assist Japan.

Japanese defence planners in recent years have consequently initiated efforts to fill any potential deterrence gap by investigating the role of a strike capability to add to deterrence by denial, or even by punishment, and raise the costs for any adversary seeking to coerce Japan or threaten its southwestern islands. Media reports, several years after the fact, revealed that the Japan Defence Agency (JDA) in 1994 had investigated the feasibility of ASDF strikes on missile bases; and in the following years senior politicians, JDA officials, and the LDP debated the value of a strike capability and its legitimacy within constitutional interpretations (Schoff and Song 2017). In 2003, Ishiba Shigeru, as Director General of the then JDA, indicated his agency had already started investigating the acquisition of the US-developed *Tomahawk*, and thus a possible strike capability. In 2017, reports from a conservative thinktank and an LDP study group proposed that Japan should develop a counterstrike ability to conduct enemy base strikes, with cruise missiles as a possible option (Japan-US Alliance Study Group 2017; Klinger 2021: 6). Following the JMOD's decision to cancel *Aegis Ashore*, Abe stated in a June 2020 press conference that the NSC should be charged with thinking in new directions about deterrence to fill the potential vacuum in defensive power (Abe 2021a). Abe was also reported to have confided in private that, 'with the advent of new [North Korean] missiles, there's a limit to what can be done with a shield. We have to have a halberd' (*The Japan News* 2020). The LDP's Subcommittee on National Defence took Abe's stance as a cue to investigate in an August 2020 report options for improving national deterrence, including alternative missile defences and strike capabilities. The report recommended that Japan should consider ways to strengthen deterrence and possessing the capability to prevent ballistic missile attacks 'within the territory of adversaries' (Jiyū Minshutō Seimuchōsakai 2020: 3) Although this oblique language was chosen to avoid controversy, it was in effect a call for a strike capability. Abe in response to the report then indicated in a September prime ministerial statement that Japan should investigate alternative national capabilities to deal with missile threats rather than sole reliance on BMD. Again, Abe employed vague language on the actual alternatives but by indicating that interception of missiles was insufficient for defensive needs the implication was that a strike capability was now on the table (Abe 2021b). Suga after taking over from Abe as prime minister proved more cautious, rolling the issue over to the next NDPG revision and wary of domestic controversy. However, Kishida in his campaign for the LDP presidency and then as prime minister during the Lower House elections in autumn 2021 touted the possibility of acquiring a strike capability and instructed the NSC in October to review the possession of this option, and it may become a major feature of the revised NSS and NDPG planned for 2022, which may clarify Japan's concept of operations for a strike (Jiyū Minshutō 2021: 35).

If Japan were to develop a strike capability it clearly still faces a wealth of issues to address beyond just political resolve. Firstly, Japan needs to clarify the operational conditions for initiating a strike. Japan's consistent stance, despite frequent domestic and international speculation otherwise, has been that it does not seek to undertake pre-emptive strikes. Japanese policymakers in the past have defined preemption as when an attack is *feared* to be imminent and argued that acting at that point would be beyond constitutional limits. Instead, the position has been that Japan can only act when an adversary has taken *actual* steps to inflict damage. Consequently, policymakers in the post–Cold War period have debated scenarios and actual steps taken by an adversary that would permit a Japanese strike, and, for instance, whether preparations for a missile attack such as fueling or raising to vertical a missile launcher would be sufficient (Schoff and Song 2017). In more recent years, however, the Japanese debate appears to be edging away from striking an enemy missile before launch, and more towards a counterattack and counter-force strategy (Schoff and Song 2017; Murano 2020). Japanese policymakers are aware that North Korea's road-mobile and solid-fuel missiles are much harder to strike at source and real-time before an attack, and that BMD capabilities may be able to absorb some initial attacks (Mori and Kitaoka 2022: 15–16). In this situation, a counter-strike capability to reduce follow-on attacks would be made more feasible both constitutionally as a clear act of self-defence and operationally as the source of attacks would be easier to identify and target.

Secondly, Japan needs to develop the hardware for any strike capability. The ASDF's stand-off missiles with their long ranges might serve this function, although Japanese policymakers have insisted these are for the defence of southwestern islands rather than striking enemy bases (Klinger 2021: 11). The JMOD is further looking to develop the GSDF's Type 12 missile to increase the range to 900 kilometres and then up to 1,500 kilometres, and with a potential aircraft-launched variant to further extend its range. The JSDF's F-35s with their stealth and air defence penetration and CEC capability might also offer a 'stand-in' capability closer to enemy targets (Murano 2020). The MSDF's new *Taigei*-class submarines with Harpoon missiles might offer a strike option, and the JMOD was reported in 2022 as looking to develop a 1,000-kilometre range submarine-launched cruise missile for striking enemy ships and land-based missiles (*Yomiuri Shimbun* 2021). As already noted, Japanese policymakers have expressed interest at times in the *Tomahawk* as a proven and relatively cheap cruise missile for a strike capability. There is even the possibility that Japan might investigate ballistic missiles to provide an even cheaper and more lethal option that can better evade air defences (Klinger 2021: 11; Murano 2020b). The JMOD will further need to integrate these types of capabilities with ISR for dynamic and persistent tracking of targets, improved command-and-control systems, and suppression of air defences. As noted in Sections 3.3

to 3.5, the JSDF is developing many of these systems through satellites and UAVs, JADGE and jointness, and electromagnetic warfare, but still has much work to deploy a complete package (Hornung 2022).

3.8 Conclusion

The JSDF in the post–Cold War period, and especially accelerating over the last decade, has indeed made significant inroads on its plans to construct a comprehensive national defence architecture as the first component of its overall security strategy. This has entailed transformation to become an increasingly formidable force characterised by a new propensity for mobility and proactivity in defensive duties, seeking to operate more effectively across all domains and the new domains of space, cyber, and electromagnetic warfare, and all in more joint fashion. The MDDF is the culmination of these converging trends. The JSDF is also increasingly unfettered in terms of constraints on doctrine and capability acquisition. Previous anti-militaristic prohibitions have been systematically abandoned.

But whilst the JSDF is undoubtedly a more capable and less constrained force all-round, it is not necessarily the case that it is becoming a more proactive military outside its traditional security responsibilities and living up to the label of a proactive contribution to peace. The JSDF, even in shifting from its Cold War stance, has prioritised instead the evolving threats from North Korea and China, and most particularly ballistic missiles, immediate maritime security needs around Japan, and territorial defence of southwestern islands. The overwhelming focus of JSDF doctrine and capability has focussed on homeland defence, and as seen in Sections 4 and 5 other security concerns have continued to play an increasingly distant consideration in the last decade. The JSDF's force structure has remained focussed on maintaining a shield function to complement US spear offensive functions to serve predominantly bilateral alliance ends. Even where there has been some shift with Japan's contemplation of its own potential spear for a strike capability, this has been developed to supplement and integrate with the United States rather than any other partner or objective. It might be argued that Japan's focus on these missions is unsurprising given the rise of China, but it does throw into sharp relief the divergence from the rhetoric of and practical limitations to the proactive contribution to peace outside homeland defence and support for US strategy.

4 US-Japan Alliance Integration

The US-Japan alliance, as the second component of national security strategy, has always been of foundational importance for Japan and in recent years has only continued to evolve and become more dominant in defence planning, and to increasingly determine and even crowd out the other key components of strategy. As noted in Section 2, policymakers in the post-war era have regarded US military hegemony as the basis for Asia-Pacific and global security – if not constituting the very international security system itself – and thus in turn establishing the indispensable frameworks for Japan's security. Japan's entire post-war grand strategy in the form of the Yoshida Doctrine, and especially in its early stages, was only made possible by the facility to outsource many defensive responsibilities to the United States. The development of Japan's defence posture thereafter was conducted with close reference to the US military commitment to Japan: first, in line with the US-Japan security treaty, and then with its morphing into the US-Japan alliance relationship, and the classic 'shield' and 'spear' bilateral division. But as outlined in Section 2, Japan's degree of dependency on the United States for military security was not always comfortably accepted nor unconditionally proffered. Japanese policymakers' concerns over alliance dilemmas of entrapment and abandonment meant they hedged their commitments to the US-Japan alliance, whether this meant at various times obfuscating Japan's degree of strategic and operational convergence with the United States or maintaining military capabilities complementary but separate from and non-integrated with US forces.

In the post–Cold War period, however, and again accelerating over the last two decades and mirroring and very much interlinked with the shift in Japan's own national defence efforts, the US-Japan alliance has undergone a process of deep transformation. The perception that the relative decline of US military hegemony is responsible for the increasing fluidity of the international security system and the rise of the challenges to Japan's security, as noted in Section 2, has convinced Japanese policymakers of the need to double down on support for the US-Japan alliance. Japan's objective has become less to avoid entrapment and increasingly to avoid risks of abandonment if the United States loses the will and capability to fulfil its security obligations to the region and thereby Japan as well.

4.1 The Evolution of the US-Japan Alliance from the Late Cold War to the 2000s

Japan shifted incrementally towards greater military convergence with the United States in the latter stages of the Cold War with the further development of the complementary but still separate 'shield' and 'spear' division of labour. As outlined in Section 2, in the post–Cold War period, highlighted on the global level by the 1990–1 Gulf War and then on the regional level by the 1994 North

Korean nuclear crisis, Japanese policymakers became starkly aware that the US-Japan alliance was not effectively oriented to respond to such challenges and overly focussed on Japan's immediate defence. In addition, the emerging issues in the mid-1990s over the disproportionate presence of US bases in Okinawa – the prefecture hosting approximately 75 per cent of US-exclusive use bases facilities in Japan that occupy around 20 per cent of its land area, despite accounting for less than 1 per cent of total national territory, and with US forces committing crimes that sparked large-scale popular protests in the prefecture – focussed Japanese and US policymakers' minds on the need to address the political and operational fragilities of the alliance. Japanese policymakers concluded it was necessary to upgrade bilateral alliance commitments to avoid risks of potential abandonment by the United States that might view Japan as an unreliable ally offering only limited capabilities to provide support in future contingencies (Tanaka 1994; Yeo 2019: 75–8).

The result was that the revised 1995 NDPG and moves to restructure Japan's defence capabilities were designed for the first time with direct reference to the US plans for reshaping its security presence in the Asia-Pacific. Japanese policymakers further responded to US alliance expectations with Prime Minister Hashimoto Ryūtarō and President Bill Clinton's announcement in April 1996 of the 'US-Japan Joint Declaration on Security: Alliance for the Twenty First Century'. The Joint Declaration stressed the importance of the bilateral alliance not just for the security of Japan, but also for the first time of the entire Asia-Pacific region; emphasised the importance of maintaining US troop levels in Japan and the region; pledged Japan's continued Host Nation Support (HNS) to support the costs of US bases in Japan; and committed Japan and the United States to cooperate in studying BMD. Simultaneous with the Joint Declaration, the United States and Japan also signed the Acquisition and Cross-Servicing Agreement (ACSA), enabling Japan to provide logistical support to the United States in peacetime exercises, international relief activities, and UNPKO. The Joint Declaration pointed significantly to the importance of interoperability in all facets of cooperation between the JSDF and US forces and committed to review the 1978 Guidelines for US-Japan Defense Cooperation (MOFA 1996).

The Defence Guidelines review was released in September 1997 and now emphasised enhanced bilateral cooperation on Article 6-type regional contingencies, the contingencies that Japan had largely avoided substantive cooperation with the United States on in the first 1978 iteration. The fields for cooperation included activities to deal with refugee flows, non-combat operations, the enforcement of economic sanctions, US forces' utilisation of JSDF and civilian base facilities, rear area support, and minesweeping – all items which the United States might have potentially requested but Japan had been unable to provide during the North Korean nuclear crisis in 1994. Japan then passed in May 1999 a Regional Contingencies Law (*shūhen jitaihō*), along with revisions to the JSDF Law, to create the legal framework to mobilise the JSDF and provide logistical support for the United States in security 'situations in areas surrounding Japan'. The SCC in 1996 also attempted to address base issues by establishing the Special Action Committee on Okinawa (SACO) to plan for return of several US facilities to the prefecture, including the relocation of the USMC Futenma air station from densely populated Ginowan City to an artificial island to be created off USMC Camp Schwab in the Henoko area of Nago City in the north of the prefecture.

Through this process of the revision of the NDPG and US-Japan Defence Guidelines, Japan started to converge with the United States strategically and operationally. Nevertheless, Japan, even in doubling down on the alliance, remained cautious to hedge commitments. Japanese policymakers insisted that the Defence Guidelines had not been designed to counter the threat from any specific country, and that the term *shūhen* was 'situational' rather than 'geographical'. The government maintained the linguistic artifice that the revised Defence Guidelines still contained a geographical element in the sense that the scope of their operation was probably relatively close to Japan and so did not necessitate a revision of Prime Minister Kishi Nobusuke's 1960 definition of the scope of the security treaty as relating to the Far East and focused on the area north of the Philippines, and South Korea, and Japan. At the same time, the introduction of 'situational' need preserved a degree of strategic ambiguity in the scope of the Defence Guidelines, with the advantage of stretching the US-Japan alliance to encompass potentially the entire Asia-Pacific but simultaneously obfuscating if Japan was committed to supporting the United States in specific contingencies such as the Korean Peninsula or Taiwan. Japan's delimiting of its military commitments was reinforced by Japanese policymakers' insistence that, running against received military rationality, the JSDF during a regional military conflict would be able to fix a line between combat zones involving US deployments and non-combat zones for JSDF supporting logistical deployments, and thus that there was no risk of the JSDF becoming embroiled and breaching the prohibition on the exercise of collective self-defence.

Japan's next step in strengthening the US-Japan alliance in response to emergent crises, US expectations for alliance support, and concerns over abandonment, came in the wake of 11 September 2001 and the 'war on terror'. To support the US-led and NATO-commanded International Security Force (ISAF) Afghanistan coalition, the Koizumi administration passed in the National Diet an Anti-Terrorism Special Measures Law (ATSML) that enabled the despatch of the MSDF to conduct non-combat refuelling operations for coalition ships in the Indian Ocean in 2002, and with successive extensions of the law and operations up until 2009. Furthermore, in response to expectations for allies' support in the US intervention in Iraq, Japan passed an Iraqi Reconstruction Law in 2003 that enabled JSDF despatch on non-combat logistical and reconstruction missions in Iraq from 2004 to 2008. Japan's defence planners feared the risks of entrapment if they provided direct military assistance for the United States in these conflicts, but at the same time were even more cognisant of the potential risks of abandonment if they were seen not to be forthcoming as a reliable ally and to 'fly the flag' and put 'boots on the ground', and feared the knock-on consequences of this for US support in Japan's own growing regional security fears regarding North Korea and China (Koizumi 2003; Sakaki, Maull, Lukner, Krauss and Berger 2020: 115–16).

Koizumi's despatch of the JSDF to the Indian Ocean and Iraq undoubtedly signalled an important development in Japan's preparedness to support its US ally. The missions in the Indian Ocean and Iraq represented the first official despatch of the JSDF during an ongoing conflict. Japan had further expanded the scope of JSDF despatch to include not just the Asia-Pacific but now extending across to the Indian Ocean and Middle East. The legislation for these missions also expanded the functional scope of JSDF despatch – differing from the IPCL and Regional Contingencies Law in that they permitted JSDF use of weapons to protect not only the lives and bodies of individual JSDF personnel and their units, but also those who 'have come under their control', interpreted as meaning wounded personnel from US and other forces, and refugees from the Afghan and Iraqi conflicts.

But once again, even as Japan inched closer to the United States in military cooperation, it maintained the predilection to hedge. Japan preserved its constitutional constraints, including the ban on the exercise of collective self-defence, in formulating the legislation for the ATSML and Iraq despatch. The ATSML provided a legal framework for JSDF despatch by making use of extant UN resolutions and then bridging these to the constitution's preamble and Japan's obligations to maintain an 'honoured place in international society'. Despatch of JSDF could then be initiated without invoking individual or collective self-defence but using instead a form of quasi-collective security that closed off any mandate for support of the United States and its coalition partners in a combat role. Japanese policymakers used a similarly ingenious artifice to enable JSDF despatch to Iraq, again predicating the 2003 Iraqi Reconstruction Law on UN resolutions and linking to the preamble of the constitution (Hughes 2004: 129–30). Japan was thus able to exercise something akin to de facto collective security in both Afghanistan and Iraq, but by stretching constitutional interpretations rather than by revision, and still with considerable hedging against the types of operations permitted for the JSDF. Japanese legislators ensured that all JSDF missions were non-combat in nature, each mission was made possible by a separate law that created firewalls between operations to avoid mission creep, and missions were timebound to enable over-lengthy commitments and withdrawals if necessary.

Japan moved closer still to the United States in the Defence Policy Review Initiative (DPRI) of the early to mid-2000s. The SCC in December and then in February 2005 agreed a set of common regional and now global objectives for the alliance (MOFA 2002, 2005a). In October 2005, the SCC laid out a set of specific areas where bilateral military cooperation would be enhanced, with a particular emphasis on improving interoperability, intelligence exchange and the sharing of base facilities (MOFA 2005b). This statement and the May 2006 US-Japan Roadmap for Realignment Implementation, and then a further May 2007 SCC Joint Statement, concluded a significant set of moves to start to integrate Japanese and US strategy and capabilities (MOFA 2006, 2007a). Japan's acceptance of the relocation of the US Army's I Corps (a rapid-deployment force with a geographical ambit covering the Asia-Pacific and the Middle East) from the continental United States to Camp Zama in Kanagawa, beginning in 2008, implied that Japan would now serve as a frontline command post for US global power projection.

Japan's relocation of the GSDF's recently formed CRF rapid-reaction force to Camp Zama between 2008 and 2012 was further aimed to strengthen interoperability between the United States and Japan. Even more significantly, Japan's agreement under the DPRI to establish a Bilateral Joint Operations Coordination Centre (BJOCC) at USAF Yokota, co-locating ASDF and US air-defence systems, increasingly entailed the sharing of sensor information and the integration of Japanese and US BMD forces (Handa 2010: 157–61). The SCC confirmed in May 2007 that the United States and Japan were committed to the 'routine sharing of BMD and related operational information directly with each other on a real-time, continuous basis' (MOFA 2007a). Japan permitted the United States to deploy additional BMD assets, including an X-band radar system at Shariki in Aomori Prefecture, PAC-3s in Okinawa, and from 2006 onwards BMD-capable *Aegis* destroyers, further deepening bilateral cooperation in this area. Japan and the United States also concluded a General Security of Military Information Agreement (GSOMIA) in 2007 to facilitate the sharing of military intelligence for BMD and defence industrial cooperation. Meanwhile, efforts were redoubled through the realignment process to seek a resolution to Okinawa base issues following considerable local political opposition to the original plans for the Futenma Replacement Facility (FRF) and US doubts over its military feasibility. The realignment roadmap indicated that 8,000 USMC personnel stationed in Okinawa would be moved to Guam and revealed a new plan for relocating the FRF to Camp Schwab itself and building two 1,600-metre additional runways on an artificial peninsula created through landfill in the adjacent bay. The Japanese government agreed to pay for all the construction costs in Okinawa and 40 per cent of the relocation costs to Guam.

Japan in yet again doubling down on alliance cooperation with the United States can thus be seen to have jettisoned previous inhibitions about overly converging and integrating strategy and capabilities with the United States. Japanese policymakers' moves in this direction under the DPRI were not absolute given that they reportedly resisted at the time a further revision of the Defence Guidelines. Moreover, US-Japan alliance cooperation encountered initially new uncertainties with the downfall from power of the LDP in 2009 and the advent of the DPJ government. Although the DPJ was arguably always highly committed to the US-Japan alliance, its early moves in government induced doubts over the solidity of the alliance (Hughes 2012; Hornung 2012). The DPJ under Prime Minister Hatoyama Yukio emphasised initially Japan building diplomatic relations with China and other states in the region to demonstrate more autonomy in foreign policy and promote multilateralism, ended the MSDF Indian Ocean despatch in 2010, and then questioned the plan for the FRF relocation within Okinawa. DPJ policymakers, facing implacable resistance from the United States, soon returned to uphold bilateral realignment plans and to emphasise even more explicitly the centrality of the US-Japan alliance (O'Shea 2014; Green 2009). In turn, the continuing rise of China and the 2010 incident around the Senkaku Islands, and then joint US-Japan efforts in *Operation Tomodachi* to respond to the Great East Japan Earthquake in March 2011, involving the mobilisation of around 20,000 US personnel and twenty USN vessels, further consolidated DPJ policymakers' conviction in the need for a strengthened bilateral alliance.

4.2 The US-Japan Alliance and the Abe Doctrine

The subsequent displacement of the DPJ from power and return of the LDP under Abe then brought about the most radical strengthening of the US-Japan alliance to date. As noted in Section 2, the Abe administration placed singular emphasis on the relative decline of the US-centred international system as accounting for the concomitant deterioration of Japan's security situation, and that the best remedy to address this and any related risks of abandonment, was to further reinvest in the alliance with the United States as the foundation of Japan's defence (Liff 2017: 158). Abe's logic held both for supporting the Obama administration's Asia pivot strategy and then for the transition to the Trump administration. For even though Trump publicly mooted perceived doubts over the continued utility of the alliance as lacking sufficient reciprocity from Japan to assist the United States in defending not just Japan but also in other regional contingencies, Abe's response was simply to further push deepening of strategic ties with the United States.

The Abe administration chose to undertake this strengthening of alliance ties by casting aside most of the constraints of post-war defence doctrine and hedging tactics vis-à-vis the alliance and to throw in its lot emphatically with its US ally (Liff 2019). These moves were tantamount to abandoning the former Yoshida Doctrine and instituting the new implicit Abe Doctrine that emphasised deeper and integrated alliance cooperation, with the aim of making Japan a truly indispensable ally that would undergird the US security presence in and around Japan, prevent Japanese abandonment, and hopefully enable Japan's treatment as a more equal ally of the United States.

Abe strengthened the alliance in two major ways. The first, drawing on the logic outlined in Section 2, that in the contemporary age no state can defend itself alone and international collective responses are indispensable, was to overturn Japan's self-imposed ban on the right of collective self-defence, essentially for the purposes of US-Japan alliance cooperation. The Cabinet Decision in May 2014 providing for significant reinterpretations of Article 9 formed the basis for an extensive range of security legislation eventually passed by the National Diet in 2015 (Cabinet Secretariat 2014). The most radical piece of legislation was the new Law on Responses to Contingencies enabling Japan's exercise of the right of collective self-defence and under 'three new conditions' (*shin-sanjōken*): where an attack on another state in a close relationship with Japan poses a clear danger of overturning the Japanese people's right to life, liberty, and the pursuit of happiness; where there is no other appropriate means to repel the attack; and where the use of force is restricted to the 'minimum necessary' to repel the attack.

The second major piece of legislation was the Law to Ensure Security in Contingencies Significantly Affecting Japan that replaced the 1999 Regional Contingencies Law and now argued Japanese logistical support would not be 'integral to the use of force' provided that the forces of other states were not actively involved in a theatre of combat. The JSDF was thus no longer limited to 'rear area' support distanced from combat zones and could instead provide support for states immediately behind their combat lines or in transit to combat theatres (Martin 2017: 479–80). The third and fourth key pieces of legislation were a new International Peace Support Law, removing the need for Japan to enact separate laws for each JSDF despatch to provide logistical support to multinational forces, and IPCL revisions to enable the JSDF during UNPKO to use force for certain duties and to protect and rescue personnel further away (*kaketsuke keigo*, or coming-to-assistance) rather than just defending close by its own personnel or UN workers.

The Abe administration argued that the 'three new conditions' still significantly circumscribed the probability and extent of Japan's involvement in collective self-defence actions in support of the United States and other states (Hosoya 2019b: 102–9). In reality, these constraints appear empty, given that the Abe administration consistently avoided defining in detail the actual conditions that form a clear danger to national existence or survival; did not make clear the threshold for deciding when there is no alternative to military action; and obfuscated definitions of the minimum use of force. The government has, therefore, retained considerable flexibility to interpret the need for military action, as it sees fit, to respond to US calls for assistance (Hughes 2017).

In conjunction with the reinterpretation of Article 9, the Abe administration had earlier moved in mid-2015 to revise the 1997 US-Japan Guidelines for Defence Cooperation, significantly expanding the potential range of support for the US military in regional contingencies. The functional range of support has been increased to now specify intelligence, surveillance, and reconnaissance, BMD, maritime security asset protection, joint use of facilities, PKO, humanitarian assistance and disaster relief, and, for the first time, cyber, and outer space (MOFA 2015). The revised Guidelines stress a concept of 'seamless cooperation' removing the rigid separation in previous guidelines of bilateral cooperation into 'Japan' and 'regional' contingencies. The intention is that military cooperation will operate smoothly across all potential scenarios and levels of conflict escalation. In turn, the revised Defence Guidelines emphasise that bilateral cooperation should now be global, and not necessarily restricted geographically, as in past formulations, to Japan itself or the surrounding region (Satake 2016: 32–3). Most significantly, the revised Defence Guidelines outline areas where the JSDF can now exercise collective self-defence with US forces, such as the protection of US shipping, interdiction of other shipping, BMD, and providing logistical support during conflicts. That the Abe administration in effect breached the ban on collective self-defence principally to support the United States was demonstrated by the fact the Defence Guidelines were agreed and released publicly before the necessary legislation had even been considered by the National Diet.

The Abe administration's doubling down on US-Japan alliance cooperation was further demonstrated by its blithe determination not only to see through the FRF plan but to speed it up in the face of continuing strong resistance within Okinawa and questions over the plan's feasibility (Hughes 2015: 68). Abe faced down two prefectural governors actively opposed to the relocation and essentially ignored a 'non-binding' referendum in Okinawa in February 2019 that with a clear majority opposed the relocation within the prefecture. In the meantime, the FRF construction project has continued despite local protests and with the timetable slipping ever backwards due to landfill technical problems. Although the Japanese government originally aimed for completion by 2022, there is now no firm date, and some estimates are for 2035 and at a cost of US$23 billion (Chanlett-Avery, Mann and Williams 2019: 3). Hence, the entire FRF project from the first creation of SACO might take nearly forty years, if completed at all.

Abe's ambitions for re-anchoring the US-Japan alliance and the US security presence in the region extended into promoting wider regional security cooperation concepts with the US-Japan relationship always at the core. Abe in his first administration was a key promoter of the Quad initiated in 2007 and involving Japan, the United States, Australia, and India. Although the Quad subsequently lost momentum, Abe in his second administration sought to revive the process with a Quad dialogue from 2017 onwards. Japan under Abe through articulating the FOIP concept also had an important impact on Trump administration strategy. The appeal of the FOIP as a vision for the Asia-Pacific for reinforcing the stability of the existing order influenced the Trump administration in developing the United States's own first Indo-Pacific Strategy in 2019, although this was cast in more overt military terms (Department of Defense 2019).

4.3 Japan's Deepening Integration with US Doctrine and Capabilities

Abe's willingness to discard Japan's constraints on bilateral cooperation set a new trajectory for the US-Japan alliance. This trend continued under Suga as his immediate successor. In certain ways, Suga, despite his diffident persona and short-lived premiership, was just as bold as Abe in pushing outwards the envelope of alliance cooperation. Suga attended the first Quad summit-level meeting in March 2021. The SCC held in the same month, the first following the formation of the two new Japanese and US administrations, reiterated the US commitment to the defence of the Senkaku Islands, opposition to any Chinese moves to change the status quo in the East China Sea and South China Sea, and support for the FOIP concept. Strikingly, the SCC joint statement referred explicitly to the importance of peace and stability in the Taiwan Strait (MOFA 2021a). The Suga-Biden summit in April and accompanying Joint Statement reiterated these positions and pledged to accelerate the strengthening of the alliance and a 'global partnership for a new era'. Japan then supported the United States to push similar phraseology regarding Taiwan in other international fora in 2021 such as the G7 (MOFA 2021b). The January 2022 US-Japan SCC statement again underscored explicitly the importance of peace and stability in the Taiwan Strait (MOFA 2022a: 2).

Japan's preparedness to identify openly the importance of Taiwan's security was a relatively new departure, given that the last US-Japan discussion at summit level was the 1969 joint communiqué between President Richard Nixon and Prime Minister Satō Eisaku that noted Taiwan was 'a most important factor for Japan's security'. Japan, as noted in Section 4.1, sought to obfuscate if the revised 1997 Defence Guidelines covered a Taiwan contingency. The February 2005 SCC did specify a peaceful resolution of issues relating to Taiwan as a 'common strategic objective' but thereafter the alliance for a decade and half avoided explicit mention of the topic (MOFA 2005a). Suga's willingness to highlight the Taiwan issue, given its extreme sensitivity for China and the possibility of feeding Sino-US conflict, thus represented even further US-Japan strategic convergence. Other Japanese policymakers are increasingly indicating that Japan may need to line up more openly with the United States in relation to the defence of Taiwan. Nakayama Yasuhide, State Minister for Defence, attracted international attention in February 2021 when he publicly termed Taiwan as a 'red line' for Japan's security; Deputy Prime Minister Asō Tarō remarked in June 2021 that an incident over Taiwan would be a threat to Japan's 'survival', evoking the language of the 2015 collective self-defence legislation, and thus Japan and the United States should work together to defend Taiwan; and Kishida during his successful run for the premiership noted in September 2021 that the situation in the Taiwan Strait was a 'big problem' for Japan (*Japan Times* 2021b). Former Prime Minister Abe upped the ante by stating in December 2021 that a 'Taiwan emergency is a Japanese emergency, and therefore an emergency for the Japan-US alliance' (*Japan Times* 2021c).

Meanwhile, Japanese leaders' determination to converge alliance interests may be given yet further impetus by the United States's precipitous withdrawal from Afghanistan in 2021. Japan has arguably more limited direct security interests in Afghanistan relating to transnational terrorism, clearly avoided the JSDF's embroilment in the conflict even at the height of the 'war on terror' by undertaking the low-risk refuelling MSDF mission, and may welcome the US withdrawal as an opportunity for it to refocus attention on the competition for influence with China in the Indo-Pacific. Nevertheless, the United States's perceived abandonment of its Afghan ally raised concerns for Japan. Biden's justification for withdrawal in Afghanistan, in that the United States feels less compulsion to support allies that are unwilling to fight for themselves, sends the signal to Japanese policymakers that to maintain the alliance there is a need for the JSDF to become even more forthcoming to support and fight alongside the United States (Kamiya 2021). Japanese policymakers may also draw similar lessons from the Ukraine crisis in that US attention and capacity could be drawn to the European theatre and away from China and Taiwan, or China observing any Russian success in its irredentist goals might be tempted to change the status quo over disputed territories in the East China Sea, and thus Japan should demonstrate that it can take up some of the burden of defence itself and provide an active backstop for maintaining the US presence in the region (*Asahi Shimbun* 2022).

The new Kishida administration appears to have made an initial response in finalising bilateral HNS negotiations at the end of 2021. Japan agreed to increase funding for US base facilities between 2022 and 2026 by around 5 per cent annually to ¥211 billion. More importantly, however, rather than the United States and Japan wrangling over the quantitative size of the increase as had occurred under the Trump administration, Japan now agreed to carve out in HNS a new 'training and equipment' category that could also fund bilateral US-Japan exercises, thus starting to shift the emphasis of HNS from 'sympathy payments' (*omoiyari yosan*) for 'compensating' US basing costs to now joint military cooperation and an 'alliance strengthening budget' (*dōmei kyōjinka yosan*) (*Asahi Shimbun* 2021).

Japanese overall investment in strategic convergence with the United States is increasingly matched by a new convergence and integration of military operational plans and capabilities, thus overcoming the previous stance of developing complementary but separate defence stances to maintain a degree of strategic autonomy. Japan's decision to procure BMD has levered open the way for the integration of bilateral capabilities and the consequent blurring of the previous distinction between Japan's defensive shield and US alliance functions.

The Japanese government in announcing its decision to introduce BMD in 2003 asserted that the system would not be used for the purpose of defending third countries and thus raised no issues of collective self-defence. However, the technological and operational logic of BMD systems, requiring real-time information sharing between Japan and the United States for any effective interception of missiles, has meant that Japan has been unable to maintain this position and progressively retreated towards de facto integration of systems with the United States. The MSDF's *Aegis* destroyers, as the mainstay of Japanese BMD providing upper-tier protection for the entire Japanese archipelago, are essentially a US-designed platform with a high degree of interoperability and data-sharing facility with the USN. In addition, the *Aegis*'s SM-3 Block IIA interceptor missile is a bilateral co-developed system. Japan has developed a range of its own FPS and space-based sensors for BMD. But the MSDF also relies on US Defence Support Program (DSP) satellites, and, most crucially on US Space Based Infrared System (SBIRS) High and Low (recently renamed the Space Surveillance and Tracking System) for infrared early-warning and off-board cueing. The MSDF also draws on sensor information provided by US forces stationed in and around the Japanese archipelago, including US X-band radars as part of the DPRI.

In turn, BMD has spelled for the first time the integration of Japanese and US command-and-control functions. The ASDF's Air Defence Command, in coordinating Japan's BMD systems through the JADGE command-and-control system, receives data relayed via the United States's Joint Tactical Ground Station (JTAGS) located at Misawa Air Base since 2007 and the United States's X-band sensors. Moreover, as noted above and part of the DPRI process, Japan integrated its BMD command-and-control functions with those of the United States through the decision to establish at USAF Yokota a collocated BJOCC for air and missile defence, a move completed by March 2012. In turn, the logic making for the convergence and eventual integration of Japan's BMD systems with those of the United States also meant that the BMD project became one of the principal justifications for Japan to breach its ban on collective self-defence for the effective operation of the system.

The shift of Japan's defence posture from providing not just a continuing defensive shield for the United States but to now the apparent fusion of capabilities and 'shield' and 'spear' functions can be seen emerging in other areas and reflecting the stated intent under the revised 2015 Defence Guidelines for bilateral 'seamless cooperation'. For instance, under the revised Defence Guidelines, Japan and the United States agreed that in the event of a contingency and damage to their respective space-based sensor systems they would offer their own capabilities to substitute for that of their alliance partner, so indicating further bilateral merging of capabilities (MOFA 2015: 21). Japan's intelligence capabilities are edging towards integration. The 2007 GSOMIA not only opened the way for enhanced information sharing with the United States on BMD and defence technology but for Japan to sign similar information sharing agreements with France in 2011, Australia in 2012, the United Kingdom in

2013, India in 2015, and South Korea in 2016. This set of agreements appears to have emboldened Japanese policymakers to speculate on joining the United States in the 'Five Eyes' intelligence sharing community, alongside the United Kingdom, Canada, Australia, and New Zealand, to become the 'Sixth Eye'. Kōno Tarō, then Minister of Defence under the Abe administration, mooted the possibility in August 2020 of Japan joining the group. The latest bipartisan report in December of the same year from Richard Armitage and Joseph Nye, influential Washington DC policymakers and 'Japan handlers', repeated the call from an earlier report for Japan to become a member of the group (Armitage and Nye 2020: 4).

4.4 First Island Chain Defence and Integrating Strike Capabilities

Japan's southwestern island defence capabilities and doctrine, as outlined in Section 3, also appear increasingly designed to integrate with and proactively support US regional military strategy for first island chain defence and including the defence of Taiwan. Japan's principal role in supporting the United States in a regional contingency remains to provide bases for US power projection and logistical rear area support. But many Japanese policymakers, even if wishing to obfuscate the reality and maintain a degree of strategic ambiguity and hedging, have long known that the United States's use of its bases in Japan to defend Taiwan would inevitably mean China seeking to strike these to hamper the US freedom of action and so draw Japan into a conflict. More recently, as noted above, Japanese policymakers have acknowledged that China's growing military potential to dominate Taiwan and in turn the maritime space around Japan and even threaten its southwestern islands mean that Japan can no longer distance itself from a conflict over Taiwan and is in effect in the very frontline along with the United States.

Deployments of the JSDF have thus now started to match this new calculation and to work in tandem with US strategy and deployments. The United States's 2018 National Defence Strategy and 2019 Indo-Pacific Strategy seek to negate China's A2/AD approach and attempts to impose *fait accompli* control on the first island chain in the Asia-Pacific through realigning certain US forward-deployed forces to the second island chain to enhance their survivability and enable long-range counterstrikes and force surges to then prevail in any conflict. At the same time, these strategies advocate maintaining sufficient forces in the first island chain for contact with, blunting, degrading, and thus denying, any rapid advances of PLA forces (Department of Defense 2018: 6–7, 2019: 18, 20–4; Townshend, Thomas-Noone and Steward 2019: 22). The expectation is that such US forces may prove sufficiently resilient to endure an initial Chinese

A2/AD assault but will also involve deployments from and greater interoperability with the forces of regional allies. Japan is clearly expected in US thinking, as the key bilateral ally in the region, with the most capable military, and interests in Taiwan's security, to anchor the topmost end of the first island chain for the United States (Mahnken, Sharp, Fabian and Kouretsos 2019: 41–2). In turn, it appears that the JSDF's southwestern island deployments, or 'wall strategy', emphasising survivability, ISR, the ability to close off surrounding sea passages to People's Liberation Army Navy (PLAN) vessels, and to then call for further support from the ARDB, MSDF, ASDF, and US forces, is in practice an integral part of this larger US first island chain and Taiwan defence strategy (Takei 2021: 6; Harold, Bansho, Hornung, Isobe, Simcock 2018: 9–12; Sacks 2022: 10–11). Japan and the United States were reported in late 2021 to be working on a joint operational plan to enable the USMC to establish an attack base in the southwest islands in a Taiwan contingency and to be supported by the JSDF (*Japan Times* 2021d). The US-Japan SCC in 2022 went some way to explicitly acknowledging this convergence of US and Japanese operational planning and forces for a Taiwan contingency, stating that the two states were making: 'robust progress ... on bilateral planning for contingencies ... to increase joint/shared use of US and Japanese facilities, including efforts to strengthen JSDF posture in areas including its southwestern islands' (MOFA 2022a: 2).

If Japan and US doctrine and capabilities are increasingly conjoined and blurred in terms of respective defensive and offensive responsibilities, then the 'shield' and 'spear' division may become even less distinct in the case of Japan's acquisition of a strike capability. Japan's interest in its own strike option might be linked to the assumption that the objective is not only to substitute for any reduced resolve or deployed capability of the United States to provide offensive power but also to then establish greater autonomy away from the alliance. Although the autonomy and hedging arguments might still carry some weight with policymakers, the dominant motivation for Japan in acquiring a strike capability is once again not to divest from the alliance but to further strengthen and invest in its credibility for deterrence. The calculation of Japan's strategic thinkers appears to be that if US deterrence were to function less readily in grey-zone contingencies and involving the southwestern islands due to these being of possibly insufficient importance to trigger an immediate US intervention and seen as primarily Japanese responsibilities, or if US forces were preoccupied in responding to other contingencies, then a Japanese strike capability would be used to supplement US capabilities and fill in gaps at the lower conventional end of the deterrence escalation ladder. Japan's willingness to mobilise a strike capability would demonstrate its resolve as an ally, prevent China from fracturing alliance unity, and make it more likely that the United States would see the utility of cooperating with Japan to counter Chinese threats (Iida 2021). Japan would thus not be looking to use its counterstrike systems, or in effect its own offensive spear, to break out of the US-Japan alliance framework, but rather to buttress the alliance and encase its smaller spear in the service of the larger spear of the United States (Murano 2020b: 68–9). Moreover, it is apparent that for any Japanese strike capability to function effectively, even though the JSDF is acquiring steadily the necessary capability, it would still need to draw on the United States for much of the information-gathering, targeting, and electronic warfare infrastructure, for learning the necessary doctrine, and for establishing a clear structure for coordinating Japanese capabilities with those of the United States (Murano 2020a; Takahashi 2006: 91–2; Hornung 2022). Furthermore, US strategic thinkers appear increasingly comfortable with the possibility that a Japanese strike capability does not necessarily prophesise Japan diverging from cooperation with the United States but signals in fact opportunities for greater bilateral integration and burden-sharing (Klinger 2021: 14; Schoff and Song 2017). Indeed, the US-Japan SCC in January 2022 acknowledged that Japanese 'capabilities to counter missile threats', or in other words a strike option, should be aligned and coordinated within broader alliance strategy (MOFA 2022a: 2).

4.5 Conclusion

The consistent pattern of Japanese approaches to the US-Japan alliance over the last three decades has been reinvesting in supporting US military power in Japan and the region. This pattern has been accentuated whenever the US presence appears under increasing challenge, or the United States indicates expectations for an enhanced Japanese contribution to the alliance. Japan has principally made enhanced contributions to the US-Japan alliance for its own immediate homeland defence and security of the immediate region. But Japan has occasionally ventured into supporting the United States further afield to bolster bilateral alliance confidence closer to home, although with seemingly limited interest in these wider US and global security interests. The other consistent pattern for Japan's periodic reinvestment in the US-Japan alliance has been that each time this commitment has become deeper with reduced hedging. The Abe Doctrine, in displacing the Yoshida Doctrine, has focussed on Japan strengthening the US-Japan alliance by accepting reduced strategic autonomy and fuller integration of the JSDF with US forces.

5 International Cooperation: Still Bilateralism-Plus

Japan's third or outer layer of security strategy, categorised as international security cooperation, and manifested in bilateral, multilateral, and institutional frameworks, is a largely new commitment in the post–Cold War period. The discourse of a proactive contribution to peace has offered expectations that Japan will expand its international security activity in terms of the geographical range and scope of activities, the number and type of country partners, and to work not only for its own security but to reciprocate support for the security ends of these partners, and that it might become less exclusively focussed on the US-Japan bilateral relationship. Japanese policymakers such as Abe have in part stoked these expectations of some type of new internationalism.

However, this section argues that even though Japan's international military cooperation marks an important shift post–Cold War and is of utility to its security strategy – especially given its near total absence of activity in this domain in the Cold War period – its overall degree of significance amongst the three components of strategy remains the most limited. This is in large part due to the need for international cooperation to be complementary and subservient to the ongoing core priorities of territorial defence and US-Japan alliance maintenance. Japan engages with new partners and multilateral frameworks in so far as they are compatible with and further those objectives, but still largely steers clear of, or keeps to a minimum, any international commitments that lie outside those immediate exigencies or might seek to infringe upon or alter them, and especially the US-Japan alliance relationship. Japan might be increasing the nominal quantity and forms of international military cooperation but the *qualitative* nature of its international security commitments and the centring of these around its ties with the United States has not substantively changed (Ruggie 1992: 566). Japan thus remains essentially on the same, even if enlarged, track of 'bilateralism-plus' it has followed since the early 2000s in this third component of security strategy (Hughes and Fukushima 2004).

5.1 UNPKO: Towards a Zero Japanese Contribution

Japan has constantly espoused UN-internationalism as one of the key pillars of its post-war diplomacy and security policy. The Basic Policy on National Defence of 1957 stated as its first principle support for the activities of the UN and promoting international collaboration to realise world peace (Asagumo Shimbunsha 2019: 27). Indeed, the fourth principle states that the US-Japan security arrangements should only be in place until such time the UN is able to respond to external aggression against Japan; and the US-Japan security treaty of 1951 and its revised version in 1960 further state that they should only remain in force up the point that the UN can satisfactorily provide for the maintenance of Japan's peace and security (MOFA 2021c).

Hence, following Japan's own stated position, any potential for the expansion of its military cooperation through the UN should be a central priority to demonstrate its commitment to international and multilateral security cooperation, and an indicator and test of its preparedness to shift away from its US-Japan alliance-oriented military strategy. But Japan, despite some early post–Cold War shifts towards enhanced UN-centred cooperation, has exercised this UN avenue for international military cooperation with declining interest in recent years, and still largely tethers its military approach towards the UN to serve the US-Japan alliance.

Japanese policymakers, to be sure, and as outlined in Section 2, have long discussed in the post-war era the importance of the UN as a form of potential military cooperation to supplement, or even substitute, for the US-Japan security relationship. In the post–Cold War period, with the potential waning of US guarantees to Japan but also concerns over entrapment, this debate intensified and the left and centrist parties, and particularly the DPJ, discussed the possibility of Japan engaging in UN-led collective security operations to now become the focal point of its international security contribution rather than through the mechanism of the US-Japan alliance (Hughes 2017: 106). Most significantly, as noted in Sections 1, 2, and 3, the JSDF made its first forays into UN-authorised missions and UNPKO. The IPCL has enabled the despatch of various UNPKO logistical and reconstruction missions, with the largest as part of UN Transitional Authority Cambodia (UNTAC) (1992–3) involving a cumulative deployment on rotation of 1,216 personnel; the UN Mission in Support of East Timor and UN Transitional Administration in East Timor (UNTAET) (2002–4) with 2,287 personnel; UN Stabilisation Mission in Haiti (MINUSTAH) with 2,184 personnel; and UN Mission in South Sudan (UNMISS) (2011–17), with 3,912 personnel (Table 2).

However, the extent to which Japan's UNPKO activities, whilst clearly involving a very valuable contribution to UN efforts for international security and carried out with professionalism by the JSDF, have effectively shifted the emphasis of its military security policy towards UN internationalism and away from US-Japan bilateralism, remains dubious. First off, even quantitatively, Japanese UNPKO despatches have been at some scale but still relatively small given the overall size of the JSDF at around a quarter of a million personnel, and with the GSDF as the prime UNPKO deployer with a total force at its disposal of around 150,000.

More important, though, is the degree of *qualitative* change that engagement in UN-authorised missions and UNPKO have engineered within Japan's overall

Table 2 JSDF overseas despatches – destination, mission, primary force, numbers of personnel

	Period of JSDF despatch	Despatch mission	Primary JSDF force despatched			Maximum number of personnel deployed at any point during mission	Cumulative total of personnel despatched across the mission
Persian Gulf	Apr 1991–Oct 1991	Logistical/reconstruction support for coalition	MSDF			510	510
Cambodia	Sep 1992–Sep 1993	UNPKO (UNTAC)		GSDF	ASDF	608	1,216
Mozambique	May 1993–Jan 1995	UNPKO (ONUMOZ)		GSDF		53	154
Rwanda	Sep 1994–Dec 1994	Refugee support			ASDF	378	378
Golan Heights	Feb 1996–Jan 2013	UNPKO (UNDOF)		GSDF		47	1,501
Honduras	Nov 1998–Dec 1998	International disaster relief			ASDF	185	185
Turkey	Sep 1999–Nov 1999	International disaster relief	MSDF			426	426
East Timor	Sep 1999–Feb 2000	Refugee support			ASDF	113	113
India	Feb 2001–Feb 2001	International disaster relief	MSDF	GSDF		94	94
Afghanistan	Oct 2001–Oct 2001	Refugee support			ASDF	138	138
Indian Ocean	Nov 2001–Nov 2007; Feb 2008–Jan 2010	Logistical/reconstruction support for coalition	MSDF			320	10,900
Timor-Leste	Feb 2002–Jun 2004	UNPKO (UNTAET/ UNMISET)		GSDF		690	2,287

Iran	Dec 2003–Jan 2004	International disaster relief			ASDF	31	31
Iraq	Jan 2004–Jul 2008	Logistical/reconstruction support for coalition		GSDF	ASDF	600	5,600
Thailand	Dec 2004–Jan 2005	International disaster relief	MSDF			590	590
Indonesia	Jan 2005–Mar 2005	International disaster relief	MSDF	GSDF	ASDF	925	925
Russia Kamchatka Peninsula	Aug 2005	International disaster relief	MSDF			346	346
Pakistan	Oct 2005–Dec 2005	International disaster relief			ASDF	261	261
Indonesia	May 2006–Jun 2006	International disaster relief		GSDF	ASDF	234	234
Nepal	Mar 2007–Jan 2011	UNPKO (UNMIN)		GSDF		6	24
Indian Ocean	Jan 2008–Feb 2010	Logistical/reconstruction support for coalition	MSDF			330	2,400
Sudan	Oct 2008–Sept 2011	UNPKO (UNMIS)		GSDF		2	12
Gulf of Somalia	Mar 2009–ongoing	Counter-piracy mission	MSDF	GSDF	ASDF	400	12,600
Haiti	Feb 2010–Jan 2013	UNPKO (MINUSTAH)		GSDF	ASDF	346	2,184
New Zealand	Feb 2010–Mar 2010	International disaster relief			ASDF	40	40
Pakistan	Aug 2010–Nov 2010	International disaster relief	MSDF		ASDF	514	514
South Sudan	Nov 2011–ongoing	UNPKO (UNMISS)		GSDF		405	3,912
Philippines	Nov 2013–Dec 2013	International disaster relief	MSDF			1,100	1,100
Malaysia	Mar 2014–May 2014	International disaster relief	MSDF		ASDF	140	140
Ghana	Nov 2014–Dec 2014	International disaster relief			ASDF	14	14
Indonesia	Dec 2014–Jan 2015	International disaster relief	MSDF			350	350
Nepal	Apr 2015–May 2015	International disaster relief			ASDF	140	140

Table 2 (cont.)

	Period of JSDF despatch	Despatch mission	Primary JSDF force despatched	Maximum number of personnel deployed at any point during mission	Cumulative total of personnel despatched across the mission
New Zealand	Nov 2016	International disaster relief	ASDF	30	30
Indonesia	Oct 2018	International disaster relief	ASDF	60	60
Sinai Peninsula	Apr 2019–ongoing	Multinational Force and Observers	GSDF	2	4
Djibouti	Nov 2019–Dec 2019	International disaster relief		230	230
Australia	Jan 2020–Feb 2020	International disaster relief	ASDF	80	80
Gulf of Aden	1 Oct 2020–ongoing	Information-gathering	MSDF	260	1,140

Source: Bōeishō (2021a: 108–11).

security strategy and military doctrine and capabilities and any diversion from the US-Japan alliance imperatives. As noted in Sections 4.1 and 5.2, Japan may have used the constitution's preamble and invoked the language of UN internationalism and UN resolutions to provide the constitutional pathway for the despatch of the JSDF to support the international coalition in the Indian Ocean and Iraq. But Japan's prime motive for and substantive role within these missions was to bolster US-Japan alliance solidarity and serve in US-led coalitions. Japanese thinking about UNPKO despatch has been influenced not just by the benefits for overall international security but just as heavily by those for the US-Japan alliance. The despatch of JSDF to MINUSTAH was in part motivated by humanitarian considerations but also the desire to demonstrate support for the United States by the DPJ government following its cessation of the refuelling mission in the Indian Ocean. The DPJ government was further motivated to despatch the JSDF to UNMISS to support the US-led strategy of state-building in the newly independent South Sudan and prevent it becoming a site for transnational terrorism (Fujishige, Uesugi and Honda 2022a: 144–5).

In terms of doctrine and capability, the JSDF has clearly been enabled, even within its constrained legal mandate for non-combat and logistical missions, to learn a considerable amount about how to work in a multilateral environment and, given the United States's reluctance often to engage itself in UNPKO, an environment that it is not necessarily dominated by the United States. The JSDF in the three decades that it has practiced UNPKO has made important strides to bring itself into line with other peacekeeping militaries by pursuing 'integration' missions to involve not just classic ceasefire monitoring but also diverse civilian-oriented tasks such as state-building (Fujishige, Uesugi, and Honda 2022: 1–12). Moreover, UNPKO have provided the rationale to further expand JSDF power projection capabilities in sealift and airlift.

Nevertheless, despite advances in Japan's capabilities to conduct UNPKO, its policymakers have displayed traditional caution if not disinterest to go beyond current limitations and more greatly stretch JSDF commitments. The JSDF has had constraints on the use of weapons during UNPKO gradually relaxed, with revisions to the IPCL in 2001 allowing the JSDF to use weapons to protect other personnel such as UN staff or NGO workers close by. But no major changes in legislation were to come until 2015, and Japan's security impetus in terms of developing doctrine and capabilities has predictably been focussed on the US-Japan alliance. The JSDF UNPKO missions were thus perceived as primarily learning grounds for the JSDF to work internationally, but still a sideshow, and a small one, relative to US-Japan bilateralism, meaning that Japan has 'punched below its weight' in this area (Aoi 2012).

The advent of the Abe administration might have been expected to shift the dial on the weight of the UN in Japan's military policy given its and subsequent administrations' discourse of a 'proactive contribution to peace' and talk of contributing personnel for international peace efforts. In fact, though, the Abe administration, despite evoking the language of internationalism and displaying some advances in Japan's ability to participate in UNPKO, largely took the same line of its predecessors in strategic motivations for participation, its overall assessment of UNPKO's place within security policy, and in the end very significantly scaled down, to the point of in effect ending, Japanese participation in UNPKO.

The NSS in its enunciation of Japan's security strategy devotes actually very limited attention to UNPKO within the third component of international security cooperation with only five mentions, although it does pledge to 'step up' its activities (Cabinet Secretariat 2013: 30). The Abe administration did make a significant move in its 2015 package of security legislation by revising the IPCL to enable the JSDF to come to the assistance of other personnel rather than just its own units; and, indeed, utilised examples of UNPKO as legitimising the need for Japan to breach its ban on collective self-defence in general (Hughes 2017: 94; Abe 2015). The GSDF had this, in effect, collective self-defence element added from late 2016 to its ongoing UNMISS despatch. In this way, the Abe administration was enabling the JSDF to potentially venture into more 'robust' UNPKO beyond integration and towards peace enforcement. But the Abe administration and its successors in the end have shown a limited motivation and appetite for UNPKO.

Japanese administrations' interest in UNPKO has been overridden by larger strategic considerations. The general trend of declining US and 'global north' willingness to commit troops to UNPKO – the United States ceasing all UNPKO deployments since May 2017 – appears to have also influenced Japanese policymakers. For Japan, UNPKO became less important as a marker of an international security contribution and instead military planning energy and capabilities could be redeployed to cope with the deteriorating security situation around its own homeland security. It is perhaps no coincidence that the Abe administration's announcement of its decision to withdraw the GSDF from South Sudan in March 2017, with withdrawal completed in May, came at the same time as the United States's own intention to pull back from UNPKO in general. The fact that the security situation in South Sudan was also deteriorating with armed clashes in the GSDF's vicinity, despite Japanese government protestations that no 'armed conflict' was occurring and thus there was no transgression of the GSDF's legal requirements to deploy under the IPCL in conditions of a ceasefire, further influenced Japanese policymakers' thinking (Mulloy 2021: 226–7). The clear concern was that the GSDF, especially with its new 'coming-to-assistance' mandate might become embroiled in combat in South Sudan. Japan's withdrawal of the GSDF thus demonstrated that, despite revisions to the IPCL to enhance its duties and capabilities for UNPKO, its willingness to undertake risks and a proactive contribution to security on behalf of the UN and outside the framework of the US-Japan alliance and its own homeland security was still highly circumscribed (Kolmaš 2019: 10–107).

Moreover, one of the considerations of the Abe administration was that any GSDF involvement in combat in South Sudan might impact negatively upon its efforts at the time to persuade the Japanese public to accept plans for constitutional revision. International security cooperation via the UN in policymakers' calculations was thus relegated far below issues of Japanese domestic politics. Furthermore, the Abe administration, as with its predecessors continued to use the banner of the UN to legitimise military operations that may serve other purposes. As part of the 2015 revisions to the IPCL, the JSDF was permitted to participate in PKO even if not under UN control. The outcome has been for the JSDF to despatch two GSDF officers to the Multinational Force and Observers (MFO) that monitors the ceasefire between Israel and Egypt (Hornung 2019). The mission is very small but indicates that Japan is again experimenting with international security cooperation that lies outside the immediate area of UN cooperation and yet draws on the legitimacy of the UN given that it is enabled legally by changes to the IPCL primarily designed for UNPKO.

The result of the Abe administration's determination to prioritise other security issues, to follow the US lead in non-participation in UN missions, and to avoid risks in UNPKO, has not been any renaissance of Japanese contribution in this area but instead to lead to the reduction of JSDF activities. As of mid-2022, Japan has no substantial UNPKO deployments and no plan for any. The totality of JSDF UNPKO deployments, out of its quarter of a million-size military, are four staff officers remaining in South Sudan. Japan's proactive contribution to peace essentially equates to zero UNPKO (Midford 2020: 716).

5.2 International Cooperation to Legitimise US-Led Coalitions and the US-Japan Alliance

Japan's propensity to utilise the justification of supporting the broader international community to further bilateral alliance goals is demonstrated in the JSDF missions to the Indian Ocean from 2001 to 2007 and then renewed from 2008 to 2010, and to Iraq from 2004 to 2008, ostensibly to support the international community engaged in the 'war on terror' and Iraqi reconstruction. These two missions still stand as two of the JSDF's longest and largest despatches, involving a cumulative total of 16,000 personnel from all three services (Table 2). These missions were also important in marking the first time in the post-war period that the JSDF, even though engaged in non-combat logistical and reconstruction activities, was despatched overseas during an ongoing conflict, thus transgressing a key post-war taboo. The JSDF furthermore supplied logistical support to and worked alongside a far wider range of militaries than ever before, including the United States, United Kingdom, Australia, France, Germany, Pakistan, Canada, New Zealand, the Netherlands, Italy, Spain, and Greece (Hughes 2004: 79–81). But even if the missions in some ways marked a departure for Japan's post-war security in opening new geographical and functional horizons for international security cooperation and involving not just the United States, and even though they utilised the rationale of a broader contribution to international peace to enable despatch, the dominant motivation for despatch and the ramifications for Japan's military posture – in classic bilateralism-plus mode – revolved firmly around US-Japan alliance needs.

As noted in Section 4, Japanese policymakers in seeking to despatch the JSDF on these missions and to facilitate the necessary legislation in the form of the ATSML and Iraqi Reconstruction Law constructed a justification drawing on extant UN resolutions that had enabled ISAF as a NATO mission and then connected these to the spirit of the constitution's preamble. In this way, Japan articulated a constitutional and legal pathway to engage in a form of de facto collective security and these international coalitions. Nevertheless, even though Japan's desire to demonstrate solidarity with the international community to combat transnational terrorism, eliminate WMD, and provide humanitarian assistance should not be dismissed, Japanese interest in these missions clearly was driven overwhelmingly by concerns of US abandonment if Japan failed to support its US ally. Prime Minister Koizumi in justifying JSDF despatch to Iraq soon revealed that demonstrating support for the United States was the prime concern, and the concern of successive LDP prime ministers to maintain the Indian Ocean despatch was essentially driven by anxieties not to alienate the United States, especially at a time of the need for US assistance for Japan to respond to North Korean provocations and the rise of China. In essence, therefore, Japan evoked the language and legitimacy of UN internationalism to help disguise the principal objective of, and de-sensitise potential opposition to, JSDF participation in a US-led multinational coalition.

In terms of the coalition operations and the impact on Japan's security strategy, these missions clearly did involve a degree of substantive international and multilateral cooperation, even if limited to non-combat operations, and so were not entirely nominal in nature. At the same time, though, it was clear that the substantive content and dynamism of the missions inevitably centred around US leadership and interests given that these were US-inspired 'coalitions of the willing'. The JSDF thus learned valuable lessons on how to work in a multinational coalition environment and build new links with other militaries. But these interactions were largely mediated through the agency of the United States, with the objective to service US-led security ends and to carry back these modes of cooperation to reinforce the US-Japan alliance itself (Asahi Shimbun Shūzaiha 2005: 13–37).

Japan's policymakers, in looking to deepen US-Japan bilateral cooperation through participation in US-led coalitions, also discovered through these despatches a useful means to wrap other essentially alliance-motivated operations within the ready legitimacy and language of the UN and international cooperation. It is notable that up until the early 2000s, JDA *Defence of Japan* white papers referred to UNPKO, the then main form of international cooperation, as 'international peace contribution' (*kokusai kōken*) or 'international peace support activities' (*kokusai heiwa iji katsudō)* (Bōeichō 1992, 1995). From the early to mid-2000s onwards, following the despatches to the Indian Ocean and Iraq, the JDA and JMOD changed the language subtly to talk of 'international peace cooperation duties' (*kokusai heiwa kyōryoku gyōmu*) that still included UNPKO but started to fold in alongside far larger US-led coalition activities, so associating both as synonymous activities under the banner term that originally drew on the internationalist legitimacy of the UN (Bōeichō 2002, 2006).

5.3 International Military Cooperation as an Extension of the US-Japan Alliance System

Japan in the last two decades has certainly embarked on an impressive expansion in bilateral and multilateral military cooperation, rather than just security dialogue, with a new range of partners within the Asia-Pacific region and extra-regionally. Japan has moved furthest so far with Australia, with the formation of an increasingly substantive and significant military relationship, or so-called 'quasi-alliance' (Wilkins 2018b). The 2007 Japan-Australia Joint Declaration on Security Cooperation affirmed the emerging 'strategic partnership' and established the intention for a broad range of security cooperation, spanning counterterrorism; disarmament and counter-proliferation of WMD; maritime and aviation security; PKO; and humanitarian-relief operations (MOFA 2007b). The Joint Declaration established a regular 2+2 mechanism for consultation between the respective foreign and defence ministers of both countries. Japan and Australia signed a bilateral ACSA in 2010, which came into force in 2013 and was revised in 2017. Japan and Australia also established in 2013 an

Information Security Agreement for sharing classified information, in 2014 an Agreement Concerning the Transfer of Defense Equipment and Technology, and in 2020 an outline Reciprocal Access Agreement (RAA) to enable two-way visits of personnel and assets and training in each other's territories. The MSDF has conducted frequent exercises with the Royal Australian Navy in Japanese and Australian waters and the South China Sea and the ASDF and Royal Australian Air Force conducted their first bilateral air combat exercises in Japan in September 2019. An MSDF destroyer in December 2021 escorted an Australian Royal Navy frigate during manoeuvres off the coast of Japan – the first time the JSDF had escorted a non-US military asset and demonstrating ambitions for deepening interoperability of the Japanese and Australian militaries.

Japan has looked to develop similar defence cooperation with India. Japan and India announced a Joint Declaration on Security Cooperation in 2008 that outlines cooperation through enhanced dialogue, military-to-military exchanges, and maritime security; concluded an Agreement on the Transfer of Defence Equipment and Technology in 2015; and a GSOMIA in 2016. The MSDF has regularly engaged in multilateral exercises with the Indian Navy but most notably the Malabar exercises in the Bay of Bengal, Philippine Sea, and off Japan's own coast. The MSDF and Indian Navy have also held frequent bilateral exercises in the Indian Ocean, Bay of Bengal, and Andaman Sea. The ASDF initiated bilateral exercises with the Indian Air Force in 2018 and planned their first air combat exercises in Japan in 2021, enabling the ASDF for the first time to train against Russian-designed Su-30 Indian fighters. The GSDF have also initiated exercises with the Indian Army in the form of the Dharma Guardian exercises held in 2018 and 2019 at the Counter Insurgency and Jungle Warfare School at Mizoram in India (Bōeishō 2021a: 78–9).

Japan has also succeeded in leading efforts for military cooperation and capacity-building with individual Southeast Asian states and especially those maritime states most wary of China (Jimbo 2021). Japan and the Philippines signed a Memorandum on Defence Cooperation and Exchanges and an Action Plan for Strengthening of the Strategic Partnership in 2015. Japan and Indonesia announced a Memorandum on Cooperation and Exchanges in the Field of Defence in 2015. In 2018, Japan and Vietnam announced the upgrade of their relationship to an Extensive Strategic Partnership for Peace. These agreements promote high-level and operational-level cooperation between Japanese military officials and their Southeast Asian counterparts. Japan has donated five TC-90 maritime-patrol aircraft to the Philippines, and in March 2019 concluded an agreement to supply spare parts for the Philippines' UH-1H helicopters.

Moreover, Japan as part of its ODA policy has continued to transfer coastguard cutters to ASEAN countries, including the Philippines, Vietnam, Malaysia, and Indonesia (Wallace 2013).

Japan has wrapped around these activities the 2016 Japan-ASEAN Vientiane Vision that seeks to bolster the role of Southeast Asian states in helping to uphold the rule of international law and maritime security through building capacity, transferring defence equipment, and undertaking joint exercises. Although the MSDF has not undertaken freedom-of-navigation operations it has begun to show ever more presence in Southeast Asia, categorised since 2019 as 'Indo-Pacific Deployments' – most notably with MSDF destroyers and submarines visiting Subic Bay in the Philippines in 2016, and visits to Cam Ranh Bay in Vietnam by an MSDF destroyer in 2016, a submarine in 2019, and then an *Izumo*-class destroyer later in the same year. The MSDF has also started to engage in a variety of multilateral naval exercises alongside Southeast Asian states, including with the Philippines in the Balikatan exercise since 2012 and Komodo exercises hosted by Indonesia since 2016, and bilateral 'friendship' naval exercises with Indonesia, Vietnam, Singapore, the Philippines, Thailand, and Malaysia (Bōeishō 2021a: 80–3).

Japan's major struggle for traction in its own region for building military cooperation has been with South Korea, despite its being identified as of importance in the NSS, sharing some similar security interests, and both states being close allies of the United States. Japan and South Korea have managed to conclude and preserve a GSOMIA since 2016, important for the exchange of information on North Korean missile launches, and to continue participation in multilateral exercises. Nevertheless, bilateral tensions over history and territory, and some strategic differences over how to respond to China's rise have stymied deeper bilateral cooperation, and trilateral cooperation with the United States despite its efforts to push for improved Japan-South Korea security ties (Green 2022: 165, 160–178). The Biden administration, though, continues to argue strongly for Japan and South Korea to build an infrastructure for bilateral security cooperation similar to that of Japan's with other US allies and partners, even explicitly singling this out as essential in its 2022 Indo-Pacific Strategy (The White House 2022: 9). The advent of the Kishida administration in 2021 and the new Yoon Suk-yeol administration in South Korea in 2022 may provide an opportunity to reset security ties.

Beyond the Asia-Pacific, Japan has pursued a similar pattern of stronger ties with France and the United Kingdom as Europe's two key military powers. Japan and France concluded an information-sharing agreement in 2011; an 'exceptional' strategic partnership in 2013 including 2+2 meetings from 2014 onwards; an agreement on the Transfer of Defence Equipment and Technology in 2016; and a bilateral ACSA in 2018 (Pajon 2018). Japan and France have explored plans for unmanned submarine technologies. The MSDF and GSDF have joined exercises with the French Navy since 2015 (Hornung 2020b: 47–9). Japan and the UK announced an agreement concerning the Transfer of Arms and Military Technologies and an Agreement on the Security of Information, essentially a GSOMIA, in 2013; a Dynamic Strategic Partnership in 2014; initiated a 2+2 process in 2015; concluded a Joint Declaration on Security Cooperation and an ACSA in 2017; and have agreed in principle in 2022 an RAA (Hornung 2020b: 20, 23, 25). Japan and the United Kingdom have established several projects for defence industrial cooperation, including most notably a programme for research into the feasibility and development of a joint new air-to-air missile (JNAAM) to integrate Japanese seeker technologies with the United Kingdom's *Meteor* missile. Japan and the United Kingdom have also expressed an interest in joint technologies for a stealth fighter, including plans to develop a joint jet engine demonstrator and advanced sensor technologies for their respective *Tempest* and F-X projects.

The JSDF has started exercises with the UK Armed Forces. The ASDF and Royal Air Force conducted their first joint exercises in Japan in 2016, and indeed the first ever for the ASDF in Japan with a partner other than the United States. The GSDF's ARDB and Royal Marines planned exercises for 2018, although these were abandoned due to typhoon conditions, and later in the same year the GSDF and British Army conducted bilateral drills in Japan. The MSDF and Royal Navy conducted their first exercises off Japan's waters in 2018. The United Kingdom as part of its 'Indo-Pacific tilt' despatched a carrier strike group that concluded its tour of the region with exercises in Japan in September 2021.

Japan has furthermore looked to strengthen relations with NATO as another out-of-area partner. Abe was the first Japanese prime minister to address the North Atlantic Council in 2007 and indicated the desire to move beyond counter-piracy, terrorism, and support for ISAF in Afghanistan and to a new phase of cooperation in peacebuilding, reconstruction, and disaster relief. Japan and NATO signed a joint political declaration in April 2013, stressing their commitment to the rules-based international order and strategic interests in the security and stability of the Euro-Atlantic and Asia-Pacific regions. In May 2014, Japan and NATO concluded an Individual Partnership and Cooperation Programme (IPCP) to strengthen high-level dialogue and defence exchanges, including participation in NATO exercises and activities in cyber-security, HADR, defence technology, and maritime security. The agreement was revised in 2018 to emphasise not only Japan participating in NATO activities but also NATO contributing assets to Japanese exercises in the Indo-Pacific

(Hornung 2020b: 78, 83, 84). Prime Minister Kishida attended the NATO summit in Madrid in June 2022 and pledged to upgrade Japan's efforts on IPCPs.

Japan has undertaken some substantive military cooperation with NATO states engaged in operations in Afghanistan through the MSDF Indian Ocean refuelling mission. In 2014, Japan became a member of the NATO Interoperability Platform, which seeks to facilitate partner cooperation in NATO-led operations and missions through using similar doctrine, standards, procedures, and equipment. The MSDF and NATO naval vessels in line with the IPCP have conducted small-scale exercises in the Gulf of Aden, Mediterranean, and Baltic Sea (Hornung 2020b: 86–7).

Japan's other major out-of-area international security cooperation has been participation in counter-piracy operations and offshoot operations around the coast of Somalia and Gulf of Aden since 2009. The MSDF was originally despatched in March 2009 under Article 82 of the SDF Law that enabled it to protect vessels under the Japanese flag or with Japanese sailors or passengers on board. The Anti-Piracy Law passed in June 2009 then allowed the MSDF to protect the vessels of countries other than Japan and become a fully independent deployer, albeit with the JCG playing a central role in enforcing the law given that Japan regards piracy as a criminal offence and matter of policing (Vosse 2021: 155–6). The MSDF has worked in coordination with the Combined Task Force 151 (CTF151) to share surveillance information and provide 'zone defence' in the Gulf of Aden for vessels and has escorted shipping under its own national auspices. The MSDF has provided commanders for the CTF151, and the MSDF has been provided with valuable opportunities to interact with several navies. The MSDF has continued to despatch at least one destroyer and two P-3Cs on counter-piracy missions. The ASDF has also deployed airlift squadrons, and the GSDF in the past the CRF to support and guard the MSDF mission. The counter-piracy mission, given its longevity at over twelve years, has become the largest in terms of the cumulative despatch of JSDF personnel involving by 2021 a total headcount of 12,600 personnel rotated through.

The JSDF very significantly has established at Djibouti international airport its first overseas military base in the post-war period, although attempts have been made to obfuscate its purpose by terming it as an 'activities hub' (*katsudō kyoten*) (Bōeishō 2020: 385). The base provides a JSDF headquarters, hangars for MSDF aircraft, and facilities for around 300 JSDF personnel, is approximately 120,000 square metres in size, and cost US$42 million to construct and another US$20 million annually for leasing and maintenance (Vosse 2021: 162). The Djibouti base is highly valuable for the JSDF, enabling interchange with other states' militaries with adjacent installations including the

United States and France; demonstrating its ability to maintain a military presence over 10,000 kilometres from Japan; and providing a facility for other missions in the region, including the ability to monitor China's own base in Djibouti and activities in the vicinity and Indian Ocean (Mason 2018: 344–5). Japan was further able to use the Djibouti base and the MSDF deployments to display indirect support for the United States's International Maritime Security Construct and Coalition Task Force SENTINEL to prevent attacks on shipping in the Persian Gulf, Gulf of Oman, Gulf of Aden, and Southern Red Sea, and aimed at deterring Iran. Japan did not participate directly in CTF SENTINEL to avoid alienating Iran with which it traditionally maintains cordial relations, but employed its assets in the region to join the US-led intelligence-gathering effort.

Japan has thus been accelerating its engagement with a variety of forms of international security cooperation, encompassing different state partners and geographical regions, bilateral and multilateral frameworks, and types of military-related activities and deployments. But how far this surge of new activity represents a fundamental qualitative departure from past strategic and military objectives, and functions outside the ambit of US-Japan bilateralism and Japan's focus on homeland security, remains questionable.

The new international security quasi-alliances and partnerships that Japan has built up still essentially appear designed to a blueprint that apes the US-Japan alliance and to ultimately reinforce wider US-led alliance structures. Japan has replicated in its bilateral ties with Australia, India, France, and the United Kingdom, largely the same model of the US-Japan alliance through a strategic declaration, 2+2 meetings, ACSAs, information security agreements, RAAs, and defence industrial cooperation, and only stopping short of an actual mutual security treaty. All the principal partners are key US allies or partners, so Japan is demonstrating minimal intention to 'decentre' from, or substitute for, the United States as the dominant security actor in the international system and its attendant alliance structures. Indeed, the fact that Japan's relations with these partners are modelled on its own with the United States and the United States's own relations with these partners, suggests these are only designed to enhance military compatibility and 'plug and play' amongst US allies and partners and with the United States itself, so assisting US plans to conjoin more effectively the spokes and cooperation amongst its allies and reinforce the traditional US-centred 'hub and spokes' military architecture in the Asia-Pacific and Indo-Pacific regions (Oros 2021: 219–20). In a sense, therefore, Japan in pursuing broader international security cooperation is furthering US objectives akin to a form of 'federated defence' or 'integrated deterrence' that may facilitate greater bilateral ties and multilateral cooperation amongst US partners and allies but is ultimately designed to once again integrate these ties with efforts to buttress the United States's central and dominant role in the region (Green, Hicks and Cooper 2014; Austin 2021; The White House 2022: 12). Japan's quiet welcome of the announcement in 2021 of the Australia-UK-US (AUKUS) trilateral security pact, and the confirmation of support in the US-Japan January 2022 SCC – another mechanism designed to bolster the US position in the region with existing alliance partners and to bring its key out-of-area UK partner more firmly into the region – again confirms Japan's desire to underpin the US-centred security system (MOFA 2022a: 2).

Similar motivations and outcomes apply to Japan's expansion of international security cooperation beyond these major partners and into other formats of multilateral security cooperation. Japan most certainly has started new forms of bilateral and multilateral military cooperation with states in Southeast Asia that would have been largely unthinkable for much of the post-war era. It cannot be doubted that these moves provide important confidence-building and reassurance that Japan has no aggressive intention against these states (Midford 2020a: 170–2). Nevertheless, the quality of bilateral cooperation remains quite 'thin' in substance, still largely focussed on dialogue, and hence no substitute for the US military presence for Japan and these states, and in many cases where cooperation has developed multilaterally this has often only been inspired by or taken place with US backing, assent, and participation (Yuzawa 2021). Many of the multilateral military frameworks and exercises that Japan has engaged in continue to feature very prominently the United States, such as the Balikatan or Komodo exercises.

Japan's reaching out to NATO is a similar case given that while it has enabled Japan to interact with and learn from a wider range of member partners it is still, in effect, even with the recent travails of the Trump administration's critique of the trans-Atlantic alliance, a US-led multilateral framework and much of the substantial cooperation that has occurred has been to support the US-led NATO coalition in Afghanistan. Japan's counter-piracy and other missions in the Gulf of Aden have provided similar valuable opportunities to interact with and learn modes of multilateral interaction from a wide range of state partners, but again there is no fundamental departure from Japan following the US lead in these areas given the United States's prominence in helping to organise and underpin these maritime activities.

Other emerging areas of Japan's international security cooperation also appear to be similarly in conformity with and contained in their extent by constant reference to the parameters set by the US-Japan alliance. Japan has built into many of its bilateral relationships information security agreements and defence industrial cooperation agreements, and its abandonment of the previous arms export ban and adoption instead of the Three Principles on the Transfer of Defence Equipment and Technology has certainly opened the way for international cooperation in this area with other partners. This could be strategically important for Japan to promote the sharing of technology and costs on the development of new defence systems, to prime Japanese arms exports, and make for some lessening of dependence on US technology and off-the-shelf imports to preserve indigenous defence production and a degree of national autonomy (Hughes 2019).

Nevertheless, Japan has proved reluctant or incapable to fully exploit the possibilities of international cooperation in defence production that suggests in any way it is looking to decentre from the United States. Japan has chosen partners for defence industrial cooperation, such as the United Kingdom, that are, of course, US allies or themselves closely integrated with US defence contractors. Moreover, Japan continues to search for a major platform to export to or co-develop wholly beyond component elements with partners such as the United Kingdom, France, and India, meaning that the bulk of its international defence technology ties remain oriented towards the United States. Indeed, Japan's large-scale procurement of the F-35, whilst offering the potential for further international cooperation with other partners in the F-35 programme, including the United Kingdom, Italy, Netherlands, Australia, Canada, Denmark, Norway, Turkey, Singapore, and Israel, is likely to deliver few such benefits. Japan as a non-development partner in the programme and only securing limited FACO for the F-35A, and buying the F-35B off-the-shelf, is in effect insulated from meaningful technological cooperation with these states. Moreover, Japan in procuring the F-35 has needed to opt into the Autonomic Logistics Global Sustainment (ALGS) system. ALGS creates under the unitary direction of the United States and prime contractor Lockheed Martin a global supply chain for the mutual provision of parts amongst those countries that deploy the F-35. Hence, Japan's procurement of the F-35, despite its being a multi-partner alliance aircraft only further moves it into closer centring on the United States (Hughes 2018: 432). Japan has also continued to rack up other foreign military sales from the United States, procuring V-22 *Ospreys*, E-2Ds, AAVs, and UAVs, and came close to acquiring *Aegis Ashore*, meaning that levels of domestically procured armaments have fallen from traditionally around 90 per cent to around 75 per cent by the mid-2010s, and so consolidating the alliance's hold on Japanese international defence equipment procurement (Hughes 2019: 425). Meanwhile, Japan's conclusion of information security agreements and interest in the Five Eyes arrangement may produce a similar outcome. For while it might provide Japan with a range of new partners, these are again all US allies, and the United States is the central coordinator of the network with asymmetric superiority over other partners in the gathering and distribution of intelligence (Samuels 2019: 258–9; Williams 2021: 110–11).

The broader elements of Japan's grand strategy and search for new security frameworks and partners also appear still fixed ultimately on shoring up the US presence in the region and thereby the US-Japan alliance and Japanese security, and totally consistent with the strategic outlook of Japanese policymakers as outlined in Section 2. The Quad has offered greater strategic and possibly maritime cooperation with Australia and India – with all four Quad states joining together in the Malabar exercises in 2020 and 2021 and for the first time since 2007 – but is still a US-led construct and means for Japan to demonstrate support for the US presence in the region. Japan has demonstrated considerable dynamism and leadership in articulating the FOIP concept and opened possibilities for a range of expanded partnerships and activities in maritime security. The concept of FOIP and the Indo-Pacific, though, clearly has an overriding objective of retying the United States into the region, and thus is seeking to buttress the dominance of the US-centred security system rather than to move away from it to any new form of regional diplomatic and security order (Koga 2020: 51, 69).

5.4 Conclusion

Japan's international security cooperation, despite expanding quantitatively in the range of partners, frameworks, activities, and geographic regions, remains qualitatively underdeveloped and still an adjunct function of Japan's own homeland security demands and the US-Japan alliance. Japan has engaged in international security cooperation to legitimise essentially US-led coalitions, to create bilateral and multilateral networks that buttress the US-dominated regional security system, but has shown limited motivation to utilise UN frameworks as an alternative, and once again used the UN as a badge to legitimise support for the United States.

In addition, it appears that not only is Japan's international security cooperation limited in scope and tied to the parameters of the US-Japan alliance it also appears to offer little in reciprocation to those partners that it has drawn into its ambit. NATO has built up expectations for Japan to function as an effective partner. But at times it appears Japan is only interested in NATO in so far as it can be drawn onside against China. Japan assiduously avoided any reciprocal military role in the NATO mission in Afghanistan itself (Yasutomo 2014: 51–3; Hornung 2020b: 90). Similarly, Japan has been effective in drawing out-of-area states into the FOIP concept, but the onus is on these states to assist Japan in responding to China rather than Japan responding to concerns in their regions.

Japan has built ties with the United Kingdom and other European states, but the expectation is for these to contribute mainly to Japan's security in its own region. This trend may be reinforced in the aftermath of Russia's invasion of Ukraine as Japan focusses on fending off Russia in its own region with little willingness to venture into NATO's traditional area of operations. Indeed, although Japan in 2022 has readily lined up with the international community to impose economic sanctions on Russia, its military contribution to the Ukraine conflict thus far has consisted of the transfer of non-lethal aid in the form of items such as helmets and flak jackets. Japan's contribution to counter-piracy in the Gulf of Aden does go beyond its own immediate security interests, but its ulterior motivation again appears to establish a foothold to monitor maritime activity in this crucial region and especially by China as its main regional concern. Japan, therefore, may not only be continuing to still practice essentially bilateralism-plus in extending its reach into new forms of international security cooperation, but simultaneously demonstrating a lack of reciprocation that may disappoint expectations of its new security partners.

6 Conclusion: Regional and Global Implications

Japan is demonstrating all the indicators of becoming a more capable military actor and of going not just regional but also global in its military profile. The prevailing debates and certainties for some regarding Japan's military trajectory increasingly fail to convince. Japan is no longer seeking a minimalist role within the US-Japan alliance, is shedding its anti-militaristic principles and norms, is not pursuing an internationalist line as the mainstay or potential alternative for its security, and not seeking any kind of strategic breakout and autonomy. Many of the existing broad categorisations of Japan's military posture, although they have value in understanding where Japan has come from and still help inform the analysis, simply no longer stack up under empirical scrutiny as explanations in their own rights for where Japan has been heading.

As the main sections of this volume have outlined in looking at the totality of Japan's military posture across JSDF new capabilities, the US-Japan alliance, and international security cooperation, it is important to recognise fundamental change occurring and move beyond past categorisations and that Japan is traversing into a new categorisation of seeking to become a more muscular military power that is now inured to the need to integrate fully into supporting US-Japan alliance objectives. This shift in posture comes with a declining inclination to hedge on alliance commitments, and a new willingness to deploy increasing alliance integration as a force multiplier for Japan's own defence and that of the immediate surrounding region. Japan is willing to venture further outwards to the Indo-Pacific, other regions, and globally for international military cooperation but only so far as compatible with US-Japan alliance objectives. Japan's planned first revision of its NSS and then the NDPG and MTDP revisions at the end of 2022 are only likely to consolidate these trends.

As this Element has noted, Japan's drive to shift its military posture arises because for its strategists and policymakers past approaches also no longer stack up to scrutiny. The Yoshida Doctrine is no longer tenable given Japan's estimations of the deteriorating security environment, expectations for Japan to undertake more responsibility for its own security and to shore up the condition of US military hegemony, and, hence, has been superseded by the new line of the Abe Doctrine. At the same time, this is not to say that the mantra of a proactive contribution to peace and talk of a multi-layered approach to military security has always been delivered in practice or lived up to the expectations generated by its rhetoric. Japan's proactivity has principally been directed, not unsurprisingly, towards looking after its homeland defence, the build-up of its own military capabilities, and strengthening the US-Japan alliance. Resultingly, the third national security strategy component of international security cooperation has been partial, at times neglected, usually subordinated to US-Japan alliance ends, and even used as cover to legitimise the bilateral alliance. Japan has thus remained in an essential mode of bilateralism-plus in international security cooperation.

The implications of Japan's fundamentally changing military posture are significant for its own security and for Asia-Pacific and global security. Although Japan and the United States clearly seek to avoid conflict with China, Japan's deepening integration into US military strategy towards China strengthens the alliance's deterrent functions but also heightens the probability of Japan's involvement in any military action over the first island chain and Taiwan. Japan is now thrust into the frontline by going beyond just the provision of US bases and logistical support to now undertaking southwestern island defence on its own and the United States's behalf to contain China's ability to manoeuvre tactically. Moreover, Japan's potential acquisition of a strike capability and its integration into the alliance ladder of deterrence means it may now perform a role in using its own offensive power to enhance the power of the US-Japan alliance to respond to China and provocations from North Korea.

More broadly beyond Japan's immediate focus on homeland security, its enhanced military doctrine and capabilities, deepening function within the US-Japan alliance, and spreading ties of international cooperation offer up the potential for Japan to play a fuller role in the Asia-Pacific, Indo-Pacific, and even into other regions. Japan's increasing willingness to become a player and part of the regional and global military architectures could provide a much-needed capacity to bolster cooperation and stability in a range of areas such as maritime security, UNPKO, peacebuilding, and HADR. Japan has to a certain extent contributed already to these missions. But Japan has been reluctant or unable to devote major policy attention or resources to these missions as they have taken a backseat to homeland security and servicing US-Japan alliance needs.

The task for many of Japan's new military partners, and perhaps for Japanese policymakers themselves, therefore, is to consider how to fully engage Japan in cooperation outside the current areas of focus and to realise more effectively the promise of a proactive contribution to peace. The patient work of European and Asia-Pacific partners may lure Japan somewhat beyond fixation on its own security issues to provide reciprocal support for security efforts in theirs and other regions. However, this effort is likely to be hard going given the strength of the US-Japan alliance imperative, the tendency for other partners to simply plug into the US security system, and Japan's own priorities.

Japan's security trajectory may only be able to shift away from ever greater convergence with the United States, and to explore instead not just complementary but also alternative frameworks that can help deliver for Japanese security, as the result of some type of fundamental rupture in the US-Japan alliance framework. If the United States were seen to be unwilling or unable to fulfil its security guarantees to Japan, either through accommodating with adversaries or maintaining insufficient capabilities in the region, then Japanese policymakers would be obliged to start to think through options. But any retreat to anti-militarism appears far-fetched, autonomy seems unattainable given the political and resource costs, and instead it might be that a mix of greater national defence efforts and international military cooperation becomes more feasible. Japan may then engage more profoundly with new bilateral partners, multilateral frameworks, and the UN. Japan could in this way become a complete rather than partial global military power, and provide a genuine and broader proactive contribution to peace and security.

References

Abe, Shinzo (2014) Press conference by the Prime Minister, 15 May, https://japan.kantei.go.jp/96_abe/statement/201405/0515kaiken.html.

Abe, Shinzō (2021a) Abe Naikaku Sōri Daijin kisha kaiken, 18 June, https://warp.ndl.go.jp/info:ndljp/pid/11547454/www.kantei.go.jp/jp/98_abe/statement/2020/0618kaiken.html.

Abe, Shinzō (2021b). Abe Naikaku Sōri Daijin no danwa, 11 September, https://warp.ndl.go.jp/info:ndljp/pid/11547454/www.kantei.go.jp/jp/98_abe/discourse/20200911danwa.html.

Anzen Hoshō Kaigi (1994) Heisei 8nen Ikō ni Kakawaru Bōei Taikō, Tokyo, https://worldjpn.grips.ac.jp/index.html.

Anzen Hoshō no Hō-teki Kiban no Saikōchiku ni Kansuru Kondankai (2008) Anzen Hoshō no Hō-teki Kiban no Saikōchiku ni Kansuru Kondankai Hōkokusho, 24 June, Tokyo, https://dl.ndl.go.jp/view/download/digidepo_3531278_po_houkokusho.pdf?contentNo=1&alternativeNo=.

Anzen Hoshō no Hō-teki Kiban no Saikōchiku ni Kansuru Kondankai (2014) Anzen Hoshō no Hō-teki Kiban no Saikōchiku ni Kansuru Kondankai Hōkokusho, 15 May, Tokyo, https://warp.ndl.go.jp/info:ndljp/pid/8833367/www.kantei.go.jp/jp/singi/anzenhosyou2/dai7/houkoku.pdf.

Anzen Hoshō to Bōeiryoku ni Kansuru Kondankai (2004) Anzen Hoshō to Bōeiryoku ni Kansuru Kondankai Hōkokusho: Mirai e no Anzen Hoshō to Bōeiryoku Bijon, Tokyo, https://dl.ndl.go.jp/view/download/digidepo_1282476_po_3.pdf?contentNo=1&alternativeNo=.

Anzen Hoshō to Bōeiryoku ni Kansuru Kondankai (2009) Anzen Hoshō to Bōeiryoku ni Kansuru Kondankai Hōkokusho, August, Tokyo, https://dl.ndl.go.jp/view/download/digidepo_3531276_po_090928houkoku_e.pdf?contentNo=1&alternativeNo=.

Aoi, Chiyuki (2012) Punching below its weight: Japan's post-Cold War expeditionary missions. In Alessio Patalano, ed., *Maritime Strategy and National Security in Japan and Britain: From the First Alliance to Post-9/11*. Leiden: Brill Books, pp. 132–56.

Arata na Jidai no Anzen Hoshō to Bōeiryoku ni Kansuru Kondankai (2010) *Arata na Jidai ni Okeru Nihon no Anzen Hoshō to Bōeiryoku no Shōrai Kōsō: Heiwa Sōzō no Kokka o Mezashite*, August, Tokyo, https://worldjpn.grips.ac.jp/documents/texts/JPSC/20100800.O1J.html.

Armitage, Richard L. and Joseph S. Nye (2020) *The US-Japan Alliance in 2020: An Equal Alliance with a Global Agenda*. Washington DC: Center for Strategic and

International Studies, https://csis-website-prod.s3.amazonaws.com/s3fs-public/publication/201204_Armitage_Nye_US_Japan_Alliance_1.pdf.

Asagumo Shimbunsha (2019) *Bōei Handobukku 2019*. Tokyo: Asagumo Shimbunsha.

Asahi Shimbun (2021) Dōmei kyōjinka yosan to kyōchō, 22 December, p. 3.

Asahi Shimbun (2022) Jimintō Chūgoku nentō no hatsugen mo: Ukuraina jōsei Senkaku, Taiwan ni tsunagaru, 23 February, p. 4.

Asahi Shimbun Shūzaiha (2005) *Jieitai Shirazaru Henyō*. Tokyo: Asahi Shimbunsha.

Austin, Lloyd (2021) Secretary of Defense remarks for the US INDOPACOM change of command, 30 April, www.defense.gov/News/Speeches/Speech/Article/2592093/secretary-of-defense-remarks-for-the-us-indopacom-change-of-command/.

Bartlett, Benjamin (2022) Cybersecurity in Japan. In Robert J. Pekkanen and Saadia M. Pekkanen, eds., *The Oxford Handbook of Japanese Politics*. Oxford: Oxford University Press, pp. 791–808.

Berger, Thomas U. (1993) From sword to chrysanthemum: Japan's culture of anti-militarism. *International Security* **17**(4), 119–50.

Bōei Mondai Kondaikai (1994) *Nihon no Anzen Hoshō to Bōeiryoku no Arikata: Nijūisseki e Mukete no Tenbō*. Tokyo: Ōkurashō Insatsukyoku, https://worldjpn.grips.ac.jp/documents/texts/JPSC/19940812.O1J.html.

Bōeichō (1992) *Bōei Hakusho 1992*. Tokyo: Ōkurashō Insatsukyoku, www.clearing.mod.go.jp/hakusho_data/1992/w1992_03.html.

Bōeichō (1995) *Bōei Hakusho 1995*. Tokyo: Ōkurashō Insatsukyoku, www.clearing.mod.go.jp/hakusho_data/1995/ara25.htm.

Bōeichō (2002) *Bōei Hakusho 2002*. Tokyo: Ōkurashō Insatsukyoku, www.clearing.mod.go.jp/hakusho_data/2002/honmon/index.htm.

Bōeichō (2004) Heisei 17nendo Ikō ni Kakawaru Bōei Taikō ni Tsuite, 10 December, https://warp.da.ndl.go.jp/info:ndljp/pid/11591426/www.mod.go.jp/j/approach/agenda/guideline/2005/taikou.html.

Bōeichō (2006) *Bōei Hakusho 2006*. Tokyo: Ōkurashō Insatsukyu, www.clearing.mod.go.jp/hakusho_data/2006/2006/index.html.

Bōeishō (2010) *Bōei Hakusho 2010*. Tokyo: Zaimushō Insatsukyoku.

Bōeishō (2020) *Bōei Hakusho 2020*. Tokyo: Zaimushō Insatsukyoku.

Bōeishō (2021a) *Bōei Hakusho 2021*. Tokyo: Zaimushō Insatsukyoku.

Bōeishō (2021b) Waga kuni no Bōei to yosan: Reiwa 4nendo gaisan yōkyū no gaiyō, 31 August, www.mod.go.jp/j/yosan/yosan_gaiyo/2022/yosan_20210831.pdf.

Cabinet Secretariat (2013) National Security Strategy, 17 December 2013, http://japan.kantei.go.jp/96_abe/documents/2013/__icsFiles/afieldfile/2013/12/17/NSS.pdf.

Cabinet Secretariat (2014) Cabinet Decision on Development of Seamless Security Legislation to Ensure Japan's Survival and Protect its People, 1 July, www.cas.go.jp/jp/gaiyou/jimu/pdf/anpohosei_eng.pdf.

Catalinac, Amy (2016) *Electoral Reform and National Security in Japan: From Pork to Foreign Policy*. Cambridge: Cambridge University Press.

Cha, Victor (2003) Multilateral security in Asia and the US-Japan alliance. In G. John Ikenberry and Takashi Inoguchi, eds., *Reinventing the Alliance: US-Japan Security Partnership in an Era of Change*. New York: Palgrave Macmillan, pp. 141–62.

Chanlett-Avery, Emma, Christopher T. Mann and Joshua A. Williams (2019) US military presence on Okinawa and realignment in Guam. *Congressional Research Service: In Focus*, 9 April, https://crsreports.congress.gov/product/pdf/IF/IF10672/3.

Department of Defense (2018) *Summary of the 2018 National Defense Strategy of the United States of America*, Washington, DC, https://dod.defense.gov/Portals/1/Documents/pubs/2018-National-Defense-Strategy-Summary.pdf.

Department of Defense (2019) *Indo-Pacific Strategy Report: Preparedness, Partnerships and Promoting a Networked Region*, Washington, DC, 1 June, https://media.defense.gov/2019/Jul/01/2002152311/-1/-1/1/DEPARTMENT-OF-DEFENSE-INDO-PACIFIC-STRATEGY-REPORT-2019.PDF.

Dobson, Hugo (2003) *Japan and United Nations Peacekeeping: New Pressures, New Responses*. London: Routledge.

Dobson, Hugo (2017) Is Japan really back? The 'Abe Doctrine' and global governance. *Journal of Contemporary Asia* **47**(2), 199–224.

Dower, John W. (1988) *Empire and Aftermath: Yoshida Shigeru and the Japanese Experience, 1878–1954*. Cambridge, MA: Harvard University Press.

Envall, H. D. P. (2020) The 'Abe Doctrine': Japan's new regional realism. *International Relations of the Asia-Pacific* **20**(1), 31–59.

Fatton, Lionel P. (2019) A new spear in Asia: why is Japan moving toward autonomous defense? *International Relations of the Asia-Pacific* **19**(2), 297–325.

Fujishige, Hiromi, Yuji Uesugi and Tomaki Honda (2022). *Japan's Peacekeeping at a Crossroads: Taking a Robust Stance or Remaining Hesitant?* New York: Palgrave Macmillan.

George Mulgan, Aurelia (2008) Breaking the mould: Japan's subtle shift from exclusive bilateralism to modest minilateralism. *Contemporary Southeast Asia* **28**(1), 52–72.

Green, Michael J. (2001) *Japan's Reluctant Realism: Foreign Policy Challenges in an Era of Uncertain Power*. New York: Palgrave Macmillan.

Green, Michael J. (2009) Tokyo smackdown. *Foreign Policy*, 23 October, https://foreignpolicy.com/2009/10/23/tokyo-smackdown/.

Green, Michael J. (2017) *By More Than Providence: Grand Strategy and American Power in the Asia Pacific Since 1783*. New York: Columbia University Press.

Green, Michael J. (2022) *Line of Advantage: Japan's Grand Strategy in the Era of Abe Shinzō*. New York: Columbia University Press.

Green, Michael J., Kathleen Hicks and Zack Cooper (2014) *Federated Defense in Asia*. Washington DC: Center for Strategic and International Studies.

Grønning, Björn Elias Mikalsen (2014) Japan's shifting military priorities: counterbalancing China's rise. *Asian Security* **10**(1), 1–21.

Grønning, Bjørn Elias Mikalsen (2018) 'Operational and industrial military integration: extending the frontiers of the Japan-US alliance', *International Affairs*, **94**(4): 755–72.

Gustafsson, Karl, Linus Hagström and Ulv Hanssen (2018) Japan's pacifism is dead. *Survival* **60**(6), 137–58.

Hagström, Linus and John Williamson (2009) 'Remilitarization', really? Assessing change in Japanese foreign security policy. *Asian Security* **5**(3), 242–72.

Hagström, Linus and Ulv Hanssen (2015) War is peace: the rearticulation of 'peace' in Japan's China discourse. *Review of International Studies* **42**(2), 1–21.

Handa, Shigeru (2010) *Bōei Yūkai: Shishin Naki Nihon no Anzen Hoshō*. Tokyo: Junpōsha.

Hanssen, Ulv (2020) *Temporal Identities and Security Policy in Postwar Japan*. New York: Routledge.

Harris, Tobias S. (2020) *The Iconoclast: Shinzō Abe and the New Japan*. London: Hurst.

Harold, Scott W., Koichiro Bansho, Jeffrey W. Hornung, Koichi Isobe, Richard L. Simcock II (2018) *US-Japan Alliance Conference: Meeting the Challenges of Amphibious Operations*, Santa Monica, CA: RAND Corporation, www.rand.org/content/dam/rand/pubs/conf_proceedings/CF300/CF387/RAND_CF387.pdf.

Hatakeyama, Kyoko (2021) *Japan's Evolving Security Policy: Militarisation within a Pacifist Tradition*. New York: Routledge.

Heginbotham, Eric and Richard J. Samuels (2002) Japan's dual hedge. *Foreign Affairs* **81**(5), 110–21.

Heginbotham, Eric and Richard J. Samuels (2018) Active denial: redesigning Japan's response to China's military challenge. *International Security* **42**(4), 128–69.

Hikotani, Takako (2017) Trump's gift to Japan. *Foreign Affairs* **96**(5), 21–7.

Hinata-Yamaguchi, Ryo (2018) Japan's defence readiness: prospects and issues in operationalizing air and maritime supremacy. *Naval War College Review* **71**(3), 41–60.

Hornung, Jeffrey W. (2012) Japan's DPJ: the party of change. *PacNet* 24, 4 April, https://csis-website-prod.s3.amazonaws.com/s3fs-public/legacy_files/files/publication/pac1224.pdf.

Hornung, Jeffrey W. (2014) Japan's growing hard hedge against China. *Asian Security* **10**(2), 97–122.

Hornung, Jeffrey W. (2019) With little fanfare, Japan just changed the way it uses its military, *The RAND Blog*, 3 May, https://www.rand.org/blog/2019/05/with-little-fanfare-japan-just-changed-the-way-it-uses.html.

Hornung, Jeffrey W. (2020a) *Japan's Potential Contributions in an East China Sea Contingency*, Santa Monica, CA: RAND Corporation, https://www.rand.org/pubs/research_reports/RRA314-1.html.

Hornung, Jeffrey W. (2020b) *Allies Growing Closer: Japan-Europe Security Ties in the Age of Strategic Competition*, Santa Monica, CA: RAND Corporation, https://www.rand.org/content/dam/rand/pubs/research_reports/RRA100/RRA186-1/RAND_RRA186-1.pdf.

Hornung, Jeffrey W. (2022) Japanese strike capabilities and the US-Japan alliance. In RAND Corporation, ed., *Japan's Possible Acquisition of Long-Range Land-Attack Missiles and the Implications for the US-Japan Alliance: Summary of a February 2021 Conference*, Santa Monica, CA: RAND Corporation, pp. 21–34.

Hosoya, Yuichi (2019a) FOIP 2.0: the evolution of Japan's Free and Open Indo-Pacific strategy, *Asia-Pacific Review* **26**(1), 18–28.

Hosoya, Yuichi (2019b) *Security Politics in Japan: Legislation for a New Security Environment*. Tokyo: Japan Library.

Hughes, Christopher W. (2004) *Japan's Reemergence as a 'Normal' Military Power*. Oxford: Oxford University Press.

Hughes, Christopher W. (2009) *Japan's Remilitarisation*. London: Routledge.

Hughes, Christopher W. (2012) The Democratic Party of Japan's new (but failing) grand strategy: from Reluctant Realism to Resentful Realism?. *Journal of Japanese Studies* **38**(1), 109–40.

Hughes, Christopher W. (2015) *Japan's Foreign and Security Policy Under the 'Abe Doctrine': New Dynamism or New Dead End?* New York: Palgrave Macmillan.

Hughes, Christopher W. (2016) Japan's resentful realism and balancing China's rise. *Chinese Journal of International Politics* **9**(2), 109–50.

Hughes, Christopher W. (2017) Japan's security trajectory and collective self-defence: essential continuity or radical change? *Journal of Japanese Studies* **43**(1), 93–126.

Hughes, Christopher W. (2018) Japan's emerging arms transfer strategy: diversifying to re-centre on the US-Japan alliance. *The Pacific Review*, **31**(4), 424–40.

Hughes, Christopher W. (2019) Japan's defence industry: from indigenisation to exploring internationalisation. In Keith Hartley and Jean Belin, eds., *The Economics of the Global Defence Industry*. New York: Routledge, pp. 396–436.

Hughes, Christopher W. (2022) Remilitarization in Japan. In Robert J. Pekkanen and Saadia M. Pekkanen, eds., *The Oxford Handbook of Japanese Politics*. Oxford: Oxford University Press, pp. 681–700.

Hughes, Christopher W. and Akiko Fukushima (2004) Japan-US security relations: toward 'bilateralism-plus'?. In Ellis S. Krauss and T. J. Pempel, eds., *Beyond Bilateralism: The US-Japan Relationship in the New Asia-Pacific*, Stanford, CA: Stanford University Press, pp. 55–86.

Hughes, Christopher W., Alessio Patalano and Robert Ward (2021) Japan's grand strategy: the Abe era and its aftermath. *Survival: Global Politics and Strategy* **63**(1), 125–60.

Iida, Masafumi (2021) China's security threats and Japanese responses, *Strategic Japan 2021*, https://csis-website-prod.s3.amazonaws.com/s3fs-public/210405_Iida_Security%20Issues.pdf?Ag0IL6LQTTMb_HXsk3XJnIDMLazbE9Bg.

Japan Ministry of Defence [JMOD] (2010) National Defense Program Guidelines for FY 2011 and beyond, 17 December, https://www.mod.go.jp/e/d_act/d_policy/pdf/guidelinesFY2011.pdf.

JMOD (2013) National Defense Program Guidelines for FY 2014 and Beyond, 17 December, https://www.mod.go.jp/j/approach/agenda/guideline/2014/pdf/20131217_e2.pdf.

JMOD (2018) National Defense Program Guidelines for FY 2019 and Beyond, 18 December, www.mod.go.jp/j/approach/agenda/guideline/pdf/20181218_e.pdf.

Japan News (2020) Smaller area of defense was key factor in halting *Aegis Ashore* deployment in Japan, 20 June, https://the-japan-news.com/news/article/0006623805.

Japan Times (2021a) Japan's GSDF to procure transport vessels amid China's rise, 14 February, https://www.japantimes.co.jp/news/2021/02/14/national/ground-self-defense-vessels/.

Japan Times (2021b) Deputy PM says Japan must defend Taiwan with US, 6 July, https://www.japantimes.co.jp/news/2021/07/06/national/taro-aso-taiwan-defense/

Japan Times (2021c) Fumio Kishida, top contender to lead Japan, warns Taiwan is 'next big problem', 3 September, https://www.japantimes.co.jp/news/2021/09/03/national/politics-diplomacy/fumio-kishida-taiwan/?utm_source=piano&utm_medium=email&utm_campaign=72&pnespid=PcIry0vsaWIAgdHjRQ4QlZkAy4iDRIrwvyit8w?utm_source=piano&utm_medium=email&utm_campaign=72&pnespid=PcIry0vsaWIAgdHjRQ4QlZkAy4iDRIrwvyit8w.

Japan Times (2021d) Invasion of Taiwan by China would be 'economic suicide' former PM Abe warns, 1 December, https://www.japantimes.co.jp/news/2021/12/01/national/abe-china-taiwan/.

Japan Times (2021e) Japan and US draft operational plan for Taiwan contingency, 23 December, https://www.japantimes.co.jp/news/2021/12/23/national/taiwan-contingency/.

Japan-US Alliance Study Group (2017) The Trump administration and Japan: challenges and visions for Japan's foreign and security policy in the new era. *Asia-Pacific Review*, **24**(1), 1–22.

Jimbo, Ken (2021) Japan's defense and security cooperation in Southeast Asia: developing security networks, capacities and institutions. In John D. Ciorciari and Kiyoteru Tsutsui, eds., *The Courteous Power: Japan and Southeast Asia in the Indo-Pacific Era*. Ann Arbor, MA: University of Michigan Press, pp. 25–53.

Jiyū Minshutō Seimuchōsakai (2020) *Kokumin o Mamoru Tame no Yokushiryokyu Kōjō ni Kansuru Teigen*, 4 August, https://jimin.jp-east-2.storage.api.nifcloud.com/pdf/news/policy/200442_1.pdf.

Jiyū Minshutō (2021) *Seiken Kōyaku Reiwa Sannen: Atarashii Jidai o Minna-san to Tomo ni*, October, https://jimin.jp-east-2.storage.api.nifcloud.com/pdf/manifest/20211018_manifest.pdf.

Jiyū Minshutō (2022) Sōgō Seisakushū 2022, Tokyo, https://jimin.jp-east-2.storage.api.nifcloud.com/pdf/pamphlet/20220616_j-file_pamphlet.pdf, p. 116.

Kallender, Paul and Christopher W. Hughes (2017) Japan's emerging trajectory as a 'cyber power': from securitization to militarization of cyberspace. *Journal of Strategic Studies* **40**(1–2), 118–45.

Kallender, Paul and Christopher W. Hughes (2019) Hiding in plain sight? Japan's militarization of space and challenges to the Yoshida Doctrine. *Asian Security* **15**(2), 180–204.

Kamiya, Matake (2021) The United States and the world in the post-Afghanistan era: the hopes and anxieties of the international community. *JIIA Strategic Comments*, 1 November, www.jiia.or.jp/en/strategic_comment/2021/11/2021-07.html#014003.

Katagiri, Nori (2020) Shinzo Abe's Indo-Pacific strategy: Japan's recent achievement and future direction. *Asian Security* **16**(2), 179–200.

Katzenstein, Peter J. and Nobuo Okawara (1993) Japan's national security: structures, norms, and policies. *International Security* **17**(4), 84–118.

Kawasaki, Tsuyoshi (2007) Layering institutions: the logic of Japan's institutional strategy for regional security. In G. John Ikenberry and Takashi Inoguchi, eds., *The Use of Institutions: The US, Japan, and Governance in East Asia*. New York: Palgrave Macmillan, pp. 77–102.

Kishida, Fumio (2021) Press conference by the Prime Minister on a meeting of the National Security Council and other matters, 19 October, https://japan.kantei.go.jp/100_kishida/statement/202110/_00015.html.

Kishida, Fumio (2022) 'Keynote address by Prime Minister Kishida at the IISS Shangri-la Dialogue', 10 June, https://www.mofa.go.jp/fp/nsp/page3e_001212.html.

Klinger, Bruce (2021) Japanese strike capabilities: security advantages for US alliance, challenges to overcome. *Backgrounder*, no. 3644, 16 August, www.heritage.org/defense/report/japanese-strike-capabilities-security-advantages-us-alliance-challenges-overcome.

Koga, Kei (2018) The concept of 'hedging' revisited: the case of Japan's foreign policy strategy in East Asia's power shift. *International Studies Review* **20**(4), 633–60.

Koga, Kei (2020) Japan's 'Indo-Pacific' question: countering China or shaping a new regional order? *International Affairs* **96**(1), 49–73.

Koizumi, Junichiro (2003) Press conference by Prime Minister Junichiro Koizumi: the Basic Plan regarding the measures based on the Law Concerning Special Measures on Humanitarian and Reconstruction Assistance in Iraq, 9 December, http://japan.kantei.go.jp/koizumispeech/2003/12/09press_e.html.

Kokka Anzen Hoshō Kaigi (2013) Kokka anzen hoshō ni tsuite, 17 December, http://www.cas.go.jp/jp/siryou/131217anzenhoshou/nss-j.pdf.

Kokka Anzen Hoshō Kaigi Kettei, Kakugi Kettei (2014) Kuni no zonritsu o mattō shi, kokumin o mamoru tame no kireme no nai anzen hoshō hōsei no seibi ni tsuite, 1 July, http://www.cas.go.jp/jp/gaiyou/jimu/pdf/anpohosei.pdf.

Kolmaš, Michal (2019) *National Identity and Japanese Revisionism: Abe Shinzō's Vision of a Beautiful Japan and its Limits*. New York: Routledge.

Le, Tom Phuong (2021) *Japan's Ageing Peace: Pacifism and Militarism in the Twenty First Century*. New York: Columbia University Press.

Liff, Adam P. (2015) Japan's defense policy: Abe the evolutionary. *The Washington Quarterly* **38**(2), 79–99.

Liff, Adan P. (2017) Policy by other means: collective self-defense and the politics of Japan's postwar constitutional reinterpretations. *Asia Policy* 24, 139–172.

Liff, Adam P. (2019) Unambivalent alignment: Japan's China strategy, the US alliance, and the 'hedging' fallacy. *International Relations of the Asia-Pacific* **19**(3), 453–91.

Liff, Adam P. (2021) Japan's defence reforms under Abe: assessing institutional and policy change. In Takeo Hoshi and Philip Y. Lipscy, eds., *The Political Economy of the Abe Government and Abenomics Reforms*. Cambridge: Cambridge University Press, pp. 479–510.

Magosaki, Ukeru (2012) *Fuyūkai no Genjitsu: Chūgoku no Taikokuka, Beikoku no Senryaku Tenkan*. Tokyo: Kōdansha Gendai Shinsho.

Mahnken, Thomas G., Travis Sharp, Billy Fabian, and Peter Kouretsos (2019) *Tightening the Chain: Implementing a Strategy of Maritime Pressure in the Western Pacific*. Washington, DC: Center for Strategic and Budgetary Assessments, https://csbaonline.org/research/publications/implementing-a-strategy-of-maritime-pressure-in-the-western-pacific/publication/1.

Martin, Craig (2017) The legitimacy of informal constitutional amendment and the 'reinterpretation' of Japan's war powers. *Fordham International Law Journal* **40**(2), 479–80.

Maslow, Sebastian (2015) A blueprint for a strong Japan? Abe Shinzō and Japan's evolving security system. *Asian Survey* **55**(4), 739–65.

Mason, Ra (2018) Djibouti and beyond: Japan's first post-war overseas base and the recalibration of risk in security enhanced military capabilities. *Asian Security* **14**(3), 339–57.

Michishita, Narushige (2022) Japan's grand strategy for a Free and Open Indo-Pacific. In Robert J. Pekkanen and Saadia M. Pekkanen, eds., *The Oxford Handbook of Japanese Politics*. Oxford: Oxford University Press, pp. 493–514.

Midford, Paul (2018) Decentering from the US in regional security multilateralism: Japan's 1991 pivot. *The Pacific Review* **31**(4), 441–59.

Midford, Paul (2020) *Overcoming Isolationism: Japan's Leadership in East Asian Security Multilateralism*. Stanford, CA: Stanford University Press.

Midford, Paul (2022) Global and regional security multilateralism in Japan's foreign policy. In Robert J. Pekkanen and Saadia M. Pekkanen, eds., *The Oxford Handbook of Japanese Politics*. Oxford: Oxford University Press, pp. 701–21.

Ministry of Foreign Affairs [MOFA] (1996), US-Japan Joint Declaration on Security: Alliance for the Twenty First Century, 17 April, https://www.mofa.go.jp/region/n-america/us/security/security.html.

MOFA (2002) Joint Statement: US-Japan Security Consultative Committee, 16 December, https://www.mofa.go.jp/region/n-america/us/security/scc/joint0212.html.

MOFA (2005a) Joint Statement of the US-Japan Security Consultative Committee, 19 February, https://www.mofa.go.jp/region/n-america/us/security/scc/pdfs/joint0502.pdf.

MOFA (2005b) Security Consultative Committee Document US-Japan Alliance: Transformation and Realignment for the Future, 29 October, https://www.mofa.go.jp/region/n-america/us/security/scc/doc0510.html.

MOFA (2006) United States-Japan Roadmap for Realignment Implementation, 1 May, https://www.mofa.go.jp/region/n-america/us/security/scc/doc0605.html.

MOFA (2007a) Joint Statement of the Security Consultative Committee. Alliance Transformation: Advancing United States-Japan Security and Defense Cooperation, 1 May, https://www.mofa.go.jp/region/n-america/us/security/scc/joint0705.html.

MOFA (2007b) Japan-Australia Joint Declaration on Security, 13 March, https://www.mofa.go.jp/region/asia-paci/australia/joint0703.html.

MOFA (2014) The Thirteenth IISS Asian Security Summit—The Shangri-La Dialogue—Keynote Address by Shinzo Abe, Prime Minister, Japan, 30 May, https://www.mofa.go.jp/fp/nsp/page4e_000086.html.

MOFA (2015) The Guidelines for Japan-US Defense Cooperation, 27 April, https://www.mofa.go.jp/files/000078188.pdf.

MOFA (2016a) Policy speech by Foreign Minister Kishida at JIIA Forum, 19 January, https://www.mofa.go.jp/fp/pp/page4e_000370.html.

MOFA (2016b) Address by Prime Minister Shinzo Abe at the opening session of the Sixth Tokyo International Conference on African Development, 27 August, https://japan.kantei.go.jp/97_abe/statement/201608/1218850_11013.html.

MOFA (2020a) Address by Prime Minister Suga at the Seventy-Fifth Session of the United Nations General Assembly, 26 September, https://www.mofa.go.jp/fp/unp_a/page4e_001095.html.

MOFA (2020b) *Japan's Efforts for a Free and Open Indo-Pacific*, May, https://www.mofa.go.jp/policy/page25e_000278.html.

MOFA (2021a) Japan-US Security Consultative Committee, 16 March, https://www.mofa.go.jp/na/st/page3e_001112.html.

MOFA (2021b) US-Japan Joint Leaders' Statement: US-Japan Global Partnership for a New Era, 16 April, https://www.mofa.go.jp/files/100177718.pdf.

MOFA (2021c) Japan-US Security Treaty, https://www.mofa.go.jp/region/n-america/us/q&a/ref/1.html.

MOFA (2022a) Joint Statement of the Security Consultative Committee (2+2), 7 January, https://www.mofa.go.jp/files/100284739.pdf, pp. 1–3.

MOFA (2022b) Japan-US Summit Meeting, 23 May, https://www.mofa.go.jp/na/na1/us/page4e_001261.html.

Mochizuki, Mike M. (2007) Japan's shifting strategy toward the rise of China. *Journal of Strategic Studies* **30**(4–5), 739–76.

Mori, Satoru and Shinichi Kitaoka (2022) The case for Japan acquiring counter-strike capabilities: limited offensive operations for a defensive strategy. In RAND Corporation, ed., *Japan's Possible Acquisition of Long-Range Land-Attack Missiles and the Implications for the US-Japan Alliance: Summary of a February 2021 Conference*, Santa Monica, CA: RAND Corporation, pp. 7–20.

Mulloy, Garren (2021) *Defenders of Japan: The Post-Imperial Armed Forces, 1946–2016*. London: Hurst and Company.

Murano, Masashi (2020a) The modality of Japan's long range strike options, policy roundtable: the future of Japanese defense and security. *Texas National Security Review*, 1 October, https://tnsr.org/roundtable/policy-roundtable-the-future-of-japanese-security-and-defense/#essay4.

Murano, Masashi (2020b) The future of deterrence strategy in long-term strategic competition. In Yuki Tatsumi and Pamela Kennedy, eds., *Key Challenges in Japan's Defense Policy*. Washington, DC: Stimson Center, pp. 61–72.

Nishikawa, Yoshimitsu (2008) *Nihon no Anzen Hoshō Seisaku*. Tokyo: Kōyō Shobō.

Oros, Andrew L. (2008) *Normalizing Japan: Politics, Identity and the Evolution of Security Practice*. Stanford, CA: Stanford University Press.

Oros, Andrew L. (2017) *Japan's Security Renaissance: New Politics and Policies for the Twenty-First Century*. New York: Columbia University Press.

Oros, Andrew L. (2021) The continued centrality of the United States to Japan's security in an era of expanding security partnerships. In Paul Midford and Wilhelm Vosse, eds., *New Directions in Japan's Security: Non-US Centric Evolution*. New York: Routledge, pp. 215–27.

O'Shea, Paul (2014) Overestimating the 'power shift': the US role in the failure of the Democratic Party of Japan's 'Asia pivot'. *Asian Perspective* **38**(3), 435–59.

Pajon, Celine (2018) A new Japan-France strategic partnership: A view from Paris. *Lettre du Centre Asie*, 74, 16 November, https://www.ifri.org/en/publications/editoriaux-de-lifri/lettre-centre-asie/new-japan-france-strategic-partnership-view.

Patalano, Alessio (2014) Japan as a seapower: strategy, doctrine, and capabilities under three defence reviews 1995–2010. *Journal of Strategic Studies* **37**(3), 403–41

Pekkanen, Saadia (2020) Japan's space power. *Asia Policy* **15**(2), 27–33.

Pugliese, Giulio and Aurelio Insisa (2017) *Sino-Japanese Power Politics: Might, Money and Minds*. New York: Palgrave Macmillan.

Pyle, Kenneth B. (2007) *Japan Rising: The Resurgence of Japanese Power and Purpose*. New York: Public Affairs Book.

Pyle, Kenneth B. (2018) *Japan in the American Century*. Cambridge, MA: The Belknap Press of Harvard University.

Ruggie, John A. (1992) Multilateralism: the anatomy of an institution. *International Organization* **46**(3), 561–98.

Sacks, David (2022) *Discussion Paper: Enhancing US-Japan Coordination for a Taiwan Conflict*. New York, Council on Foreign Relations, https://cdn.cfr.org/sites/default/files/report_pdf/Enhancing%20U.S.-Japan%20Coordination%20for%20a%20Taiwan%20Conflict_DP_1.pdf.

Sakaki, Alexandra, Hanns W. Maull, Kerstin Lukner, Ellis S. Krauss and Thomas U. Berger (2020) *Reluctant Warriors: Germany, Japan and Their US Alliance Dilemma*. Washington, DC: Brookings Institution Press.

Samuels, Richard J. (2003) *Machiavelli's Children: Leaders and their Legacies in Italy and Japan*. Ithaca, New York: Cornell University Press.

Samuels, Richard J. (2006) Japan's Goldilocks strategy. *The Washington Quarterly* **94**(4), 111–27.

Samuels, Richard J. (2007) *Securing Japan: Tokyo's Grand Strategy and the Future of East Asia*. Ithaca, New York: Cornell University Press.

Samuels, Richard J. (2013) *3.11: Disaster and Change in Japan*. Ithaca, New York: Cornell University Press.

Samuels, Richard J. (2019) *Special Duty: A History of the Japanese Intelligence Community*. Ithaca, New York: Cornell University Press.

Satake, Tomohiko (2016) The new Guidelines for Japan-US Defence Cooperation and an expanding Japanese security role. *Asian Politics and Policy* **8**(1), 27–38.

Satake, Tomohiko and Ryo Sahashi (2021) The rise of China and Japan's 'vision' for a Free and Open Indo-Pacific. *Journal of Contemporary China* **30**(127), 18–35.

Schoff, James and David Song (2017) Five things to know about Japan's possible acquisition of strike capability. Carnegie International Endowment for Peace, 17 August, https://carnegieendowment.org/2017/08/14/five-things-to-know-about-japan-s-possible-acquisition-of-strike-capability-pub-72710.

Singh, Bhubhindar (2008) Japan's security policy: from a peace state to an international state. *The Pacific Review* **21**(3), 303–25.

Singh, Bhubhindar (2020) *Reconstructing Japan's Security Policy: The Role of Military Crises*. Edinburgh: Edinburgh University Press.

Smith, Sheila A. (2019) *Japan Rearmed: The Politics of Military Power*. Cambridge, MA: Harvard University Press.

Soeya, Yoshihide (2005) *'Midoru Pawā' Gaikō: Sengo Nihon no Sentaku to Kōsō*. Tokyo: Chikuma Shinsho.

Suga, Yoshihide (2020) Address by Prime Minister Suga at the Seventy-Fifth Session of the United Nations General Assembly, 26 September, https://www.mofa.go.jp/fp/unp_a/page4e_001095.html.

Takahashi, Sugio (2006) Dealing with the ballistic missile threat: whether Japan should have a strike capability under its exclusively defense-oriented policy. *NIDS Security Reports*, September, 7, http://www.nids.mod.go.jp/english/publication/kiyo/pdf/bulletin_e2006_4_takahashi.pdf.

Takao, Yasuo (2008) *Is Japan Really Remilitarising? The Politics of Norm Formation and Change*. Monash: Monash University Press.

Takei, Tomohisa (2021) Daiichi rettōsen no yokushiryoku: kaiyō jōkyō haaku, 25 May, https://www8.cao.go.jp/space/comittee/27-anpo/anpo-dai43/siryou2.pdf.

Tanaka, Akihiko (1997) *Anzen Hoshō*. Tokyo: Yomiuri Shimbunsha.

Tanaka, Hitoshi (1994) Kitachōsen kakugiwaku mondai o kenshō suru. *Gaikō Fōramu*, 7, 59–64.

Townshend, Ashley, Brendan Thomas-Noone and Matilda Steward (2019) *Averting Crisis: American Strategy, Military Spending and Collective Defence in the Indo-Pacific*, August, United States Studies Centre, University of Sydney, https://www.ussc.edu.au/analysis/averting-crisis-american-strategy-military-spending-and-collective-defence-in-the-indo-pacific.

Vosse, Wilhelm (2021) Is Japan's engagement in counter-piracy missions a step towards decentering of its security policy? In Paul Midford and Wilhelm Vosse, eds., *New Directions in Japan's Security: Non-US Centric Evolution*, New York: Routledge, pp. 154–74.

Wallace, Corey J. (2013) Japan's strategic pivot south: diversifying the dual hedge. *International Relations of the Asia-Pacific* **13**(3), 488–95.

White House (2022) *Indo-Pacific Strategy of the United State*s. Washington, DC, February.

Williams, Brad (2021) *Japanese Foreign Intelligence and Grand Strategy: From the Cold War to the Abe Era*. Washington, DC: Georgetown University Press.

Wilkins, Thomas S. (2018a) Japan's new grand strategy: 'proactive realism' in the face of an 'increasingly severe security environment'. In Hidekazu Sakai and Yoichiro Sato, eds., *Re-Rising Japan: Its Strategic Power in International Relations*. New York: Peter Lang, pp. 25–62.

Wilkins, Thomas S. (2018b) After a decade of strategic partnership: Japan and Australia 'decentering' from the US alliance? *The Pacific Review* **31**(4), 498–514.

Yasutomo, Dennis T. (2014) *Japan's Civil-Military Diplomacy: The Banks of the Rubicon*. New York: Routledge.

Yeo, Andrew (2019) *Asia's Regional Architecture: Alliances and Institutions in the Pacific Century*. Stanford, CA: Stanford University Press.

Yomiuri Shimbun (2021) Dokuji: Kaiji sensuikan ni 1000kiro shatei missairu . . . tekikichi kōgekiryoku no gutaika de kentō, 30 December 2021, https://www.yomiuri.co.jp/politics/20211229-OYT1T50258/.

Yuzawa, Takeshi (2021) From a decentring and recentering imperative: Japan's approach to Asian security multilateralism. In Paul Midford and Wilhelm Vosse, eds., *New Directions in Japan's Security: Non-US Centric Evolution*. New York: Routledge, pp. 131–53.

Acknowledgements

I started work on this Element in early 2021 in the middle of the United Kingdom's second national lockdown during the COVID-19 pandemic. The opportunity to oblige myself to set aside time to write was a welcome occasional distraction from helping to lead my university's institutional efforts to design and deliver online teaching and learning during the pandemic. It also gave me a chance to refocus on many of the Japanese security debates that I had found it difficult to engage with and write about for a couple of years due to the weight of administrative duties.

I would like to thank Mary Alice Haddad, Erin Chung, and Ben Read as the series editors for suggesting that I write on this topic and helping me throughout the process of bringing the Element to fruition. I apologise to the editors for requiring a couple of extensions to the original schedule. Hopefully, though, the eventual publication of the Element is well timed given its emergence in the midst of an even more vigorous debate on military issues in Japan in 2022.

I would also like to thank a range of colleagues who were not directly involved in the development of this Element, but I was able to listen to and be stimulated by due to the strange result of the pandemic enabling me to reconnect with many academic seminars and debates globally through the new prevalence of video conferencing. I am grateful to Max Warrack, Giulio Pugliese and Veronica Barfucci for their thoughtful reading and comments on the original manuscript. The anonymous review process yielded useful insights and areas for improvement. I owe a debt of gratitude to my superb colleagues in the Education Executive at Warwick who at times served as something of a support network during the darkest days of responding to the pandemic's challenges to education and for our students.

Above all, though, I want to thank my family, Chiyako, Eleanor, and William, to whom I dedicate this Element for as always supporting me when trying to focus on writing and just in putting up with me in general.

Chris Hughes
Pro-Vice-Chancellor (Education) and Professor
of Japanese Studies and International Politics
University of Warwick

Cambridge Elements ☰

Politics and Society in East Asia

About the Series

The Cambridge Elements series on Politics and Society in East Asia offers original, multi-disciplinary contributions on enduring and emerging issues in the dynamic region of East Asia by leading scholars in the field. Suitable for general readers and specialists alike, these short, peer-reviewed volumes examine common challenges and patterns within the region while identifying key differences between countries. The series consists of two types of contributions: 1) authoritative field surveys of established concepts and themes that offer roadmaps for further research; and 2) new research on emerging issues that challenge conventional understandings of East Asian politics and society. Whether focusing on an individual country or spanning the region, the contributions in this series connect regional trends with points of theoretical debate in the social sciences and will stimulate productive interchanges among students, researchers, and practitioners alike.

Cambridge Elements

Politics and Society in East Asia

Elements in the Series

The East Asian Covid-19 Paradox
Yves Tiberghien

State, Society and Markets in North Korea
Andrew Yeo

The Digital Transformation and Japan's Political Economy
Ulrike Schaede, Kay Shimizu

Japan as a Global Military Power: New Capabilities, Alliance Integration, Bilateralism-Plus
Christopher W. Hughes

A full series listing is available at: www.cambridge.org/EPEA

Printed in the United States
by Baker & Taylor Publisher Services